MEMORIES OF HASLAR

D

MEMORIES OF HASLAR

Staff and patients write about Britain's best-loved hospital

Compiled by Eric Birbeck MVO and David Gary

CHAPLIN BOOKS
www.chaplinbooks.co.uk

First published in 2017
This edition published in 2019 by Chaplin Books

Design by Michael Walsh at The Better Book Company
Optimised and distributed by Andrews UK Limited

Chaplin Books
5 Carlton Way
Gosport PO12 1LN
Tel: 023 9252 9020
www.chaplinbooks.co.uk

Contents

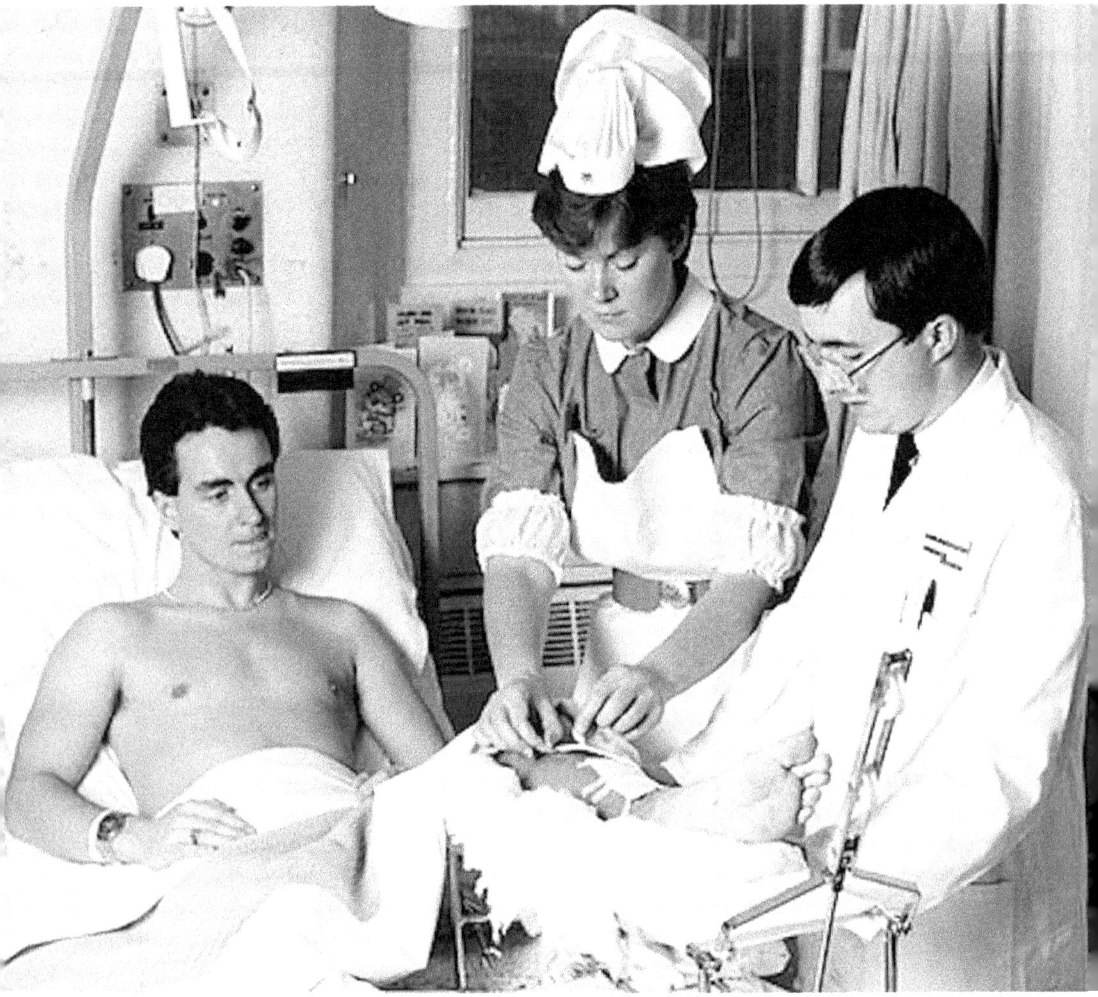

Nurse Gill Forty and Medical Technician Peter Thompson attending to a patient

FOREWORD

I first walked through the gates of Haslar in 1964 as a raw recruit to the Royal Navy Medical Service. Haslar was to remain my 'alma mater' for over 32 years: I then spent a further twelve years in a civilian technical role – and because of my role in Haslar Heritage, some say I never left.

The place was always humming with activity: from the footsteps of matrons and staff walking the wards, the voices of visitors and patients attending clinics, the squeaking of trolley wheels as patients were wheeled into theatre, the clattering of saucepans in the galley and the laughter from the pay-night 'bops' at the Haslar Club, to the whispering of nurses getting back late after a night out and the singing of the choir in St Luke's church on Sundays.

Now, all has fallen silent. From my desk in the office of Haslar Heritage Group – currently based in St Luke's Church – I can look out into the grounds, where the loudest sound is the falling of a leaf, the patter of a fox as it trots by, or the swish of a new resident's car as it passes. The wards and corridors are eerily quiet. But the sounds of a busy hospital will never fade away: they are embedded in the walls and they exist in the memories of so many people.

I have been overwhelmed by the way people responded when I told them we were putting together a book of Haslar memories. Everyone had a story to tell – nurses, medical assistants, surgeons, admin staff, ground-workers, blacksmiths, carpenters, choirboys, patients, volunteer guides, and radio station presenters. Together, their memories span seven decades, from World War II to the day that Haslar closed.

Many of the stories made me laugh out loud – such as the way Admiral Cunningham was mistaken for an Able Seaman because his initials happened to be 'AB' – and quite a few brought a tear to my eye, such as the way one patient described his nurse as his 'sheet anchor' because she'd taken the time to listen to his World War II tales: he continued to call out for her long after she had been transferred to Stonehouse.

What shines through all the memories gathered in this book is the warmth everyone felt towards Haslar: it truly was Britain's best-loved hospital.

Eric Birbeck MVO

Medical branch staff pictured in 1910

Chapter One
'The Noblest Of Institutions'

Haslar was described by Queen Victoria on one of her many visits to the hospital while staying at Osborne House as the 'noblest of institutions'. 'It would be difficult,' she said, 'to think of a hospital more loved than the Royal Hospital Haslar.'

Some of the great London hospitals have earlier foundations, but Haslar's story within British military history is unique. The 8,000 – 20,000 bodies that lie buried in its Paddock bear testimony to Britain's global reach since the 1750s.

Haslar and its clinicians made a considerable contribution to medical advances over the centuries, not just in medicine, science and research, but in geographic exploration too.

In the twentieth and early twenty-first centuries, Haslar was known for its wards with gleaming floors, immaculate bed-linen and dedicated medical and civil staff, so it is hard to believe on opening in 1753, all was not well in England's first naval hospital.

*

In 1713 an enterprising man by the name of Nathaniel Jackson, who owned the Fortune Hospital on the site of Forton Barracks, convinced the Admiralty to let him treat sick and wounded sailors for profit.

It did not prove easy, however, to transfer patients from their ships, which were often moored at Spithead. The transport service was 'contracted out' but not all of the contractors turned out to be reliable. One, a Mr Dods, took the sick to his house on the Point at Portsmouth, instead of to the Fortune Hospital. This, together with other problems, convinced the Admiralty to build their own Naval hospital at Portsmouth – plus others at Chatham and Plymouth. The Portsmouth hospital was to be placed at the point of the harbour on the Gosport side, on a 62-acre site known as Hazel Wood (the name Haslar may well be a derivative of this) and was to be designed by Theodore Jacobsen, who also designed the Foundling Hospital in London.

The cost of building Haslar was to be £38,000 for a hospital able to accommodate 1,500 patients, allowing four feet of space between beds. Work started in 1745, and by 1753 the first patients were being admitted, even though construction work was still underway. By the time it was finished in 1762, Haslar was the largest red brick building in the country (it kept the local brick kilns in Fareham and the surrounding area busy for years). It had also overshot its budget by nearly £100,000, but the result was a larger hospital than had been originally planned: there were 114 wards with a capacity of just over 2,000 beds. It was named Royal Hospital Haslar.

The position of the hospital certainly made it an easy transfer for patients arriving by boat off Spithead, but access to the town of Gosport was another matter. Until 1795, when a substantial bridge was built, the only route was via a track across the mouth of Haslar creek, often impassable due to the tide and mud. The bridge allowed all sorts of trade to take place and added to the economic viability of Gosport. Indeed, Haslar became a major employer with its laundry workers, blacksmiths, porters, cooks, stewards, security staff, vets, and carpenters. Many local craftsmen had worked on the building of the hospital, too.

Haslar's first physician was Dr George Cuthbert, who had to be persuaded to take the job: rumour has it that he did not relish the idea of starting such a large hospital from scratch. He did not stay long and was succeeded in 1758 by Dr James Lind, later considered the 'father' of nautical medicine and a pioneer in the treatment of scurvy.

Most patients were admitted suffering from fever, tuberculosis (then called 'phthisis'), or scurvy. From the very start, Haslar encouraged patients to 'take the air' as a cure, and sea bathing was also recommended.

Dr James Lind, the 'father' of nautical medicine (left) and Theodore Jacobsen, designer of Haslar (right)

The early decades at Haslar were not without problems: nurses smuggled alcohol into the hospital, hiding it in pigs' bladders under their skirts and creeping in through the hospital sewers at low tide. James Lind held enquiries and many nurses were dismissed. The patients, being mainly 'pressed men', escaped from the hospital in large numbers, necessitating a guard of soldiers to patrol the perimeter wall. Indeed, at this time Haslar resembled a prison more than a hospital: records show that all the doors on the ground floor were locked at night.

Despite the size of the hospital, it soon became overcrowded: discharged pensioner sailors lived in the attics, and staff and their families shared the main building. In 1761 three patients petitioned the Admiralty to complain at the way in which they were being mistreated by the staff, one nurse even having drawn a knife and threatened murder. Admiralty inspections followed and in the late eighteenth century Haslar underwent many changes, including the appointment of a Naval Commanding Officer as Governor in 1795, which bought about a century of change.

*

Georgian houses at Haslar, built in 1756

In the early days, Haslar's role was mainly one of caring for the sick of the Fleet and those injured in wars and sea battles. Nursing was often provided by the widows and mothers of seaman, offering what little comfort they could. Amputations were carried out in wards, often with people sleeping in the next bed and it wasn't until 1910 that the first purpose-built operating theatre was commissioned. More sailors died from infection than from any wound, with gangrene being a potential killer, and tuberculosis a close second.

During the nineteenth and early twentieth centuries many physicians travelled abroad from Haslar as members of various expeditions, not only pushing forward the frontiers of medicine but also those of global exploration. The most famous of these was Sir John Richardson, Inspector of Hospitals and Fleets, who undertook two Arctic expeditions in support of Sir John Franklin in search of the Northwest Passage – a sea route between the northern Atlantic and Pacific oceans. As well as being a naval surgeon, Richardson became a naturalist of renown, and played a part in maintaining and expanding Haslar's museum and library that held a large collection of anatomical specimens, animals and birds.

Richardson is also known to have met and corresponded with Florence Nightingale, who wished to understand how naval hospitals were run and equipped in order to improve Army hospitals, and with Charles Darwin. While Richardson was not a theorist, his findings made Darwin's theories possible.

Other Haslar physicians who went on to travel the world included Thomas Huxley, who left Haslar in 1846 to become the surgeon on board HMS *Rattlesnake* and during

Haslar labourers in the 1930s.
The only one not wearing a hat is the dog

his time in the southern hemisphere studied marine life; William Balfour Baikie, who was appointed to the Niger expedition in 1854 that explored the west coast of Africa and was instrumental in discovering a treatment for malaria; and Edward Atkinson, vaccinator at Haslar, who became Captain Scott's Medical Officer on the ill-fated South Pole expedition of 1912 – he survived and saved the expedition.

In 1847 Captain Sir Edward Parry, the renowned Arctic explorer and navigator, took command of Haslar. Parry worked with Richardson to improve the care of patients at the hospital, especially those incarcerated in the asylum that had been added in August 1818 and also the general administration of the hospital. Parry only stayed until 1852 and his departure was greatly lamented by the staff and patients of the time. His obituary mentions that on Sundays he went into the wards with his Bible to read to patients; similarly, his wife visited the asylum often and read to its inmates.

In 1884 the Royal Naval Sick Berth Branch was formed, with Sick Berth Attendants being trained to serve in naval hospitals, including Haslar. This was also the year that the first Naval Nursing Sisters, with a Head Sister in overall charge, were appointed to the Royal Naval Hospitals at Haslar, Plymouth and Chatham. Initially, the arrival of the Nursing Sisters was resented by some medical officers and male nursing staff, but very soon improvements in nursing care and the teaching of the Royal Naval Sick Berth Attendants were noted. In 1902 Queen Alexandra, wife of King Edward VII, gave her patronage to the Naval Nursing Sisters and their title then became Queen Alexandra's Royal Naval Nursing Service (QARNNS).

Louisa Hogg, Head Sister (centre) with her Nursing Sisters in 1889

In 1884 a tramway was built, running from the Haslar jetty to the central arcade of the hospital, so that patients could be transported direct from their ships. Staff had to push the ambulance carts on the tracks up the slight incline to the hospital. The tramway was used until 1920.

At the close of the nineteeth century, Haslar had acquired more new buildings, including a 'Zymotics' hospital for patients suffering from infectious diseases such as scarlet fever and tuberculosis. Zymotics stood by the sea wall with pavilions and open balconies for patients: it could be isolated from the rest of the hospital and had its own galley and stores, with an administration block topped by a clock and weather vane. In later years it was to serve as the office of the Senior Officer of the Medical Services and then the Haslar estate office with blacksmith's and carpenter's workshops.

Other nineteenth century additions include the water tower, whose water tanks could hold 50,000 gallons, a much more efficient means of providing the hospital with water than the wells that preceded; a new pathology block built away from the 'uniform line' of the other buildings so as to gain sunlight all day for lighting the microscopes; a chapel of rest and mortuary; a laundry; a Medical Mess and a QARNNS Nursing Sister mess.

Women continued to form a growing part of Haslar's staff. In 1909 the Voluntary Aid Detachment was formed, with VADs serving throughout the Royal Navy, including at Haslar; and 1917 saw the formation of the WRNS, thus bringing with it female Sick Berth Attendants.

Above: Patients during the Great War enjoying summer sunshine and fresh air. The practice went on until the 1960s.

Below: Medical Mess Officers' Stewards in the Edwardian period

The QARNNS Sisters' rose garden (see page 48 to learn more about the work undertaken by Dame Matilda Goodrich for the gardens)

Wreath-bearers at the 2005 plaque-unveiling
eremony in the Memorial Gardens to all who were
buried in the Paddock between 1753 and 1826

The social centre of Haslar was the Errol Hall, opened in 1913 as the result of a bequest from the widow of Commander George Errol, who had died in service. The main hall was regularly used for the entertainment of patients and staff. The BBC Light Programme broadcast from the hall featuring many famous acts of the day including Arthur Askey, Cyril Fletcher and Flanagan & Allen. At Christmas time pantomimes were staged and many a pop concert and dance was held: Joe Brown and the Bruvvers, and the Bay City Rollers were two of the acts who appeared. In later years the Hall became a gymnasium complete with sauna.

One of the most striking features of Haslar is the Canada Block. In 1916 the Admiralty was approached by a Canadian women's organisation, the Imperial Order of the Daughters of the Empire, who wished to donate 100,000 Canadian dollars to build a hospital ship in gratitude for care given to their troops within Europe. The Admiralty advised that the money would be better spent in support of Haslar, because Sick Berth staff were still living in the main building and really needed an accommodation block of their own. Canada Block was opened by Queen Mary on 9 May 1917 and remained in use as accommodation right up until the closure of Haslar.

*

Admiral's Walk: a VAD and her patient pose for the camera in the much-loved Quadrangle during the Great War

During the wars of the twentieth century, and especially in the Great War and World War II, Haslar was a busy hospital, caring for sailors from multi-national navies and at times for prisoners-of-war too. This meant a huge increase in staff and training.

Throughout World War II, Allied and enemy troops were treated at Haslar in great numbers: in the early war years it was treating 5,000 patients a year, but this rose to

Night duty Sick Berth Attendants, pictured in 1928

16,000 in the later years. Each patient was categorised on admission and daily thereafter by the medical officer in charge of the ward and a daily 'state' showed the number of cases fit for transfer to the cellars and elsewhere and those unfit to leave in any circumstances. Many who had undergone operations were sent to other hospitals to recover, freeing up beds for new admissions. This triage was the brainchild of US Army Surgeon Brigadier Elliot Cutler, working with Surgeon Rear Admiral Sir Cecil Wakeley. Brigadier Cutler was subsequently awarded the OBE by King George VI for his services to the UK forces.

During the war, Haslar was supposed to have 38 medical officers, 14 more than normal, but at D Day, numbers had dropped to 35, and five of these were then dispatched to Landing Craft. An urgent case was made regarding the shortage and numbers were barely made up in time.

Haslar was designated as a 'port hospital' for Gosport. Port hospitals were meant to receive only those cases so seriously wounded that they could not be transferred further inland. Therefore the bed complement for Haslar was cut from 1,100 beds to just 400. Patients then had to be transferred further inland once considered fit to travel and were sent on ambulance trains from Gosport railway station, which had been partially blitzed in previous air-raids.

One major building lost to enemy action was the Haslar museum, which had been founded in 1827 and over the years had housed thousands of artefacts collected by Naval surgeons and returned to Haslar for display from around the globe. Part of the main collection had been removed in 1855 and sent to London museums but in October 1941 the museum and its contents were destroyed by a stick of bombs from German warplanes on their way to attack Portsmouth Dockyard. One VAD, during a later visit to

Haslar, recalled that staff were encouraged to search the surrounding area for shattered remains of exhibits, some of which were hanging from trees. They were also urged to hunt for the four-footed duck that had been part of the Ornithology collection.

During the Falklands War, in 1982 many injured naval personnel were sent to Haslar for treatment. Patients were collected in ambulance buses from RAF stations at Brize Norton and Lyneham.

*

Following the inception of the National Health Service in 1948, Haslar made 84 beds available for the treatment of civilian patients: this number was to increase through the years until closure.

Haslar continued to grow in professional and technological ability in the treatment of its patients, both at home and in areas of conflict. In April 1950 the Royal Navy School of Physiotherapy opened at Haslar, including a new fully equipped physiotherapy treatment centre. In 1958 civilian students were also admitted to the School.

In 1954 the word 'Naval' was formally included in the title of the hospital, only to be removed again in 1996 when Haslar became a Tri-Service (Navy, Army and RAF) hospital and the original title of 'Royal Hospital' was reverted to once more.

In 1957 many of the wards underwent major refurbishment: roofs were replaced and the attics stripped out and refurbished. Gone

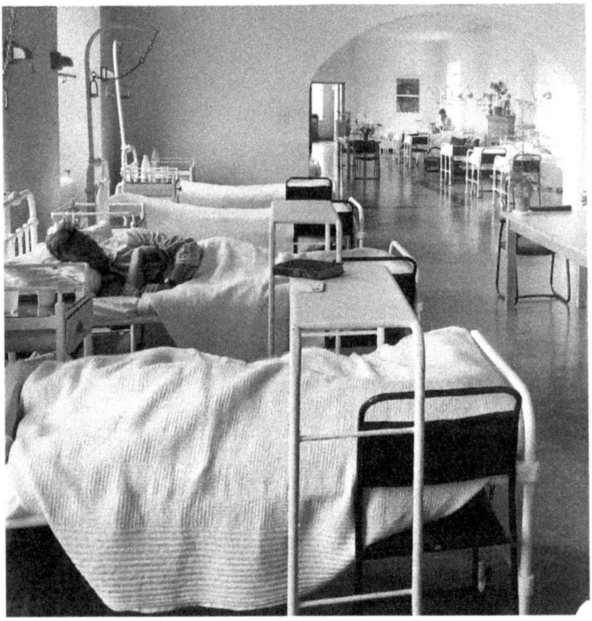

(Above): Sick Berth staff pictured in 1949. (Right): A ward in the 1950s or 1960s

were the old wooden beams that had come from ship's hulks when the hospital was first built. Along with the new iron-framed roof structures, metal window frames replaced the old Georgian sash windows, though not on the front façade, as Haslar was a listed building. Another major change was the installation of an oval staircase in what was 'B' Block: this was not universally liked, as when descending the stairs, you could see right down to the basement from the second floor – which made many feel queasy. The stairs, however, were much admired by architectural students and photographed on many occasions by visitors.

In 1967 a new Hyperbaric Unit was opened in the old original operating theatre, bringing a new medical treatment for patients with gangrene and divers with the bends. Eventually this was replaced in 1995 by a laboratory with a six-man chamber: it saved many lives of divers and those suffering from carbon monoxide poisoning.

In 1969/1970 what was known as 'A' block underwent major change; the two blocks were joined up and the ground floor now included a Post Office, NAAFI shop, telephone exchange, bank and barber's shop. Later, in 1998, the whole block was once again overhauled with a new Clinical Measurements, Dental Department, Day Surgery – including two new operating theatres – Gastroenterology departments and Nuclear medicine.

At this time, staff were permitted to use the cellar under the then 'C' Block as a folk club, which became known as the C Minus 1 Club and proved very popular. Jasper Carrott appeared there in the very early days of his career. The club only lasted a few years and eventually closed when the new Haslar club opened in 1976.

In September 1970, the Royal Naval Medical Service received the Freedom of the Borough of Gosport.

In 1976 the tennis courts, rose gardens and old Post Office were demolished. Sadly that included the cycle sheds, so the younger members of staff lost their favourite canoodling spot. Other changes including the building of a new Senior Rates mess, including a new galley supplying a cafeteria for patients and staff.

The Prince of Wales talking to Surgeon Captain Ian Jenkins in March 1999, when the Prince pushed the button on a new state-of-the-art scanner

BUCKINGHAM PALACE
LONDON SW1A 1AA

As Patron of Queen Alexandra's Royal Naval Nursing Service, I have many fond memories of visiting the Royal Naval Hospital Haslar.

I first visited on the 28th May 1957 and, since then, have had the pleasure of meeting staff and patients over many years, culminating in my last visit to Gosport on the 8th June 2000.

Alexandra

Probationary Naval Nurse Hill presents a posy to HRH Princess Alexandra on her visit to Haslar on 23 May 1969, while Miss C Thompson looks on

Above: QARNNS nurses in their walking-out uniform and beret.
Below: The refurbishment of B Block in 1957

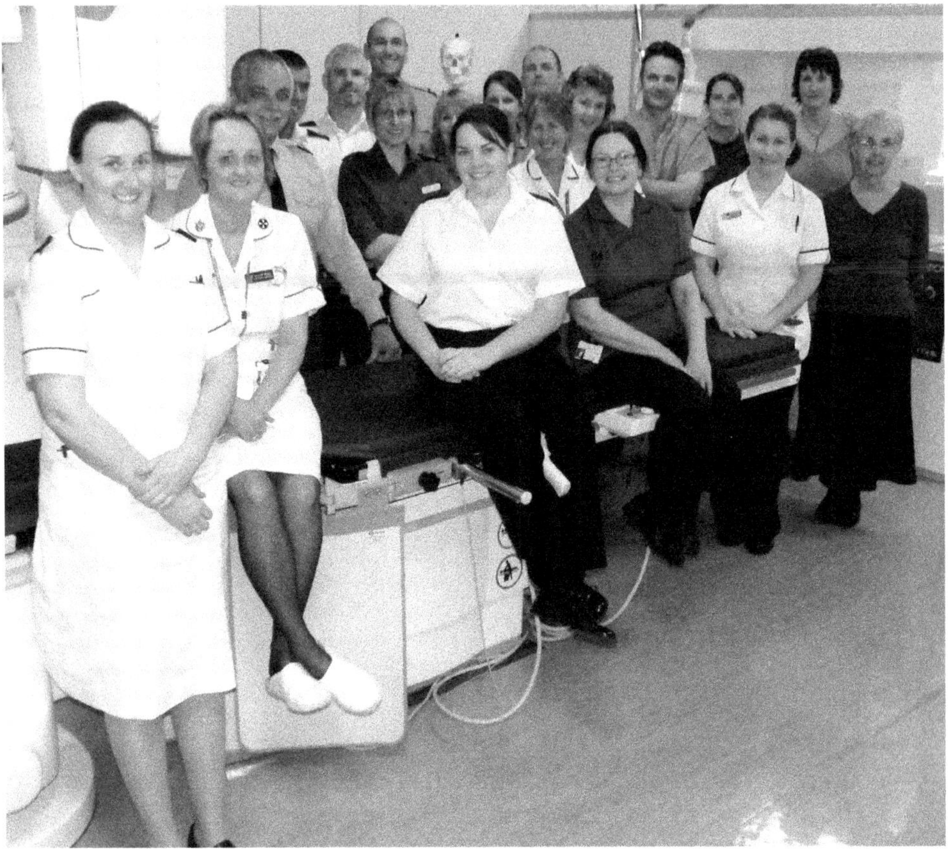

The radiology Tri-Service team: note the skeleton in the back row

The greatest building change was to take place in 1980 with the clearance of the much-loved Quadrangle with its lawns and rose beds, in order to make way for the building of the 'Crosslink', which enabled patients and staff to travel from one side of the hospital to the other under cover. This controversial building, which had large sail-like fixtures on the roof, accommodated an Accident and Emergency department, five large modern operating theatres, and a large Radiology (X-ray) department.

In addition to its medical staff, Haslar by now employed around 300 civilians – all MOD civil servants – in a great variety of roles including administrators, gardeners, laundry workers, porters, blacksmiths, chefs, galley staff, and drivers.

*

In 1996 it was decided that only one tri-Service hospital should serve the UK – and that the existing three single-Service hospitals could compete to be chosen. Haslar's case was judged to be the most persuasive and later that year it became a tri-Service hospital, with its name reverting to 'Royal Hospital Haslar'.

Concerns about its long-term future were raised in 1998 because the strategic aim was to use military medical personnel out 'in the field' and to treat patients who needed hospital care through the NHS. At the time, acute care services were being provided both at Haslar and at QA, but changes to funding meant that all acute clinical care moved to QA, and Haslar quickly lost its role as a trainer of acute care specialists – a status that was vital in providing the core skills for military medics working 'in the field'. To maintain and develop their skills, they had to move to QA or to another NHS hospital, and this accelerated Haslar's decline.

Clearly, a hospital-focused Centre for Defence Medicine was needed which would provide the right training and ethos to deliver world-class medics who could be deployed on military operations. The thinking was that this should be in partnership with a suitable NHS Trust, and an open tender was announced, to which – much to the surprise of many in the Ministry of Defence – Portsmouth Hospitals Trust decided not to respond. The tender was won by the University Hospital Birmingham Foundation Trust and it became the receiving hospital for military casualties from across the globe.

On 10 December 1998 the Government announced that it was to withdraw military forces from Haslar and to close the hospital within two years. In fact, it took much longer than that and was still functioning after a further 10 years. At the time of the decision, Haslar was said to be treating 110,000 patients a year, plus 27,000 in Accident and Emergency. Its Commanding Officer was Surgeon Captain James Campbell and it was part of the Defence Medical Education and Training Agency headed by Surgeon Rear Admiral Philip Raffaelli.

The decision to close Haslar provoked both anger and sadness in Gosport. The decision robbed the town and its 80,000 inhabitants of any meaningful Accident and Emergency cover, the nearest being 15 miles away in Cosham through very crowded roads. The people of Gosport did not take the decision lying down. The then MP, Peter Viggers, took a delegation to 10 Downing Street with 50,000 signatures, and in January 1999 – at the initiative of Gosport Borough Council and led by Cllr Peter Edgar – some 22,000 people marched through the town in protest, the largest demonstration in the UK over the closure of a hospital.

Immediately after the march, the Save Haslar Task Force felt there were encouraging signs from the government regarding the future of the hospital, but after further meetings it became clear that it saving it was unlikely. A sustained campaign did ensure it stayed open until new facilities for both military and civilians were in place.

Haslar finally closed its doors in July 2009 and the site was put up for sale. Discouraged by being told that the site had a 'book value' of £55 million, Gosport Borough Council did not bid for it, only to discover that the site was eventually sold for £3 million, to a newly formed company called Our Enterprise Haslar Ltd – later called Haslar Developments Ltd – who intended to redevelop it as housing under the 'Royal Haslar' name.

Haslar's rich heritage lives on in a number of ways. In 2001 the Haslar Heritage Group was formed, initially to organise celebrations for the hospital's 250th anniversary – including the filming of Antiques Roadshow by the BBC at Haslar in 2003. Since then, the group has continued to research, archive and display historical material associated with Haslar, to organise tours, and to support the media in producing radio and TV documentaries. The Group has also built a large international following through social media.

Haslar Heritage is now affiliated with the National Museum of the Royal Navy and the Queen Alexandra's Royal Naval Nursing Service archive. The Group plans to become a charity and form a historical archive for visitors in a building within the grounds given to them by the owner.

Above: Eric Birbeck (left) with ceramics specialist Henry Sandon at the BBC Antiques Roadshow in 2003. Henry is holding a Haslar mug.
Below: Proms in the Park with the Royal Marine Band in 2006

The Memorial Gardens continue to live on, too. Used as a cemetery until 1859, they are now cared for by 'Shore Leave at Haslar', a project for ex-Service veterans with mental health support needs. Veterans are supported by volunteers through horticultural therapy to make this garden a magical place to recuperate. The garden is a hidden gem, a combination of beautiful parkland, flower beds, vegetable beds – and bees.

Eric Birbeck and David Gary

Haslar's Grip

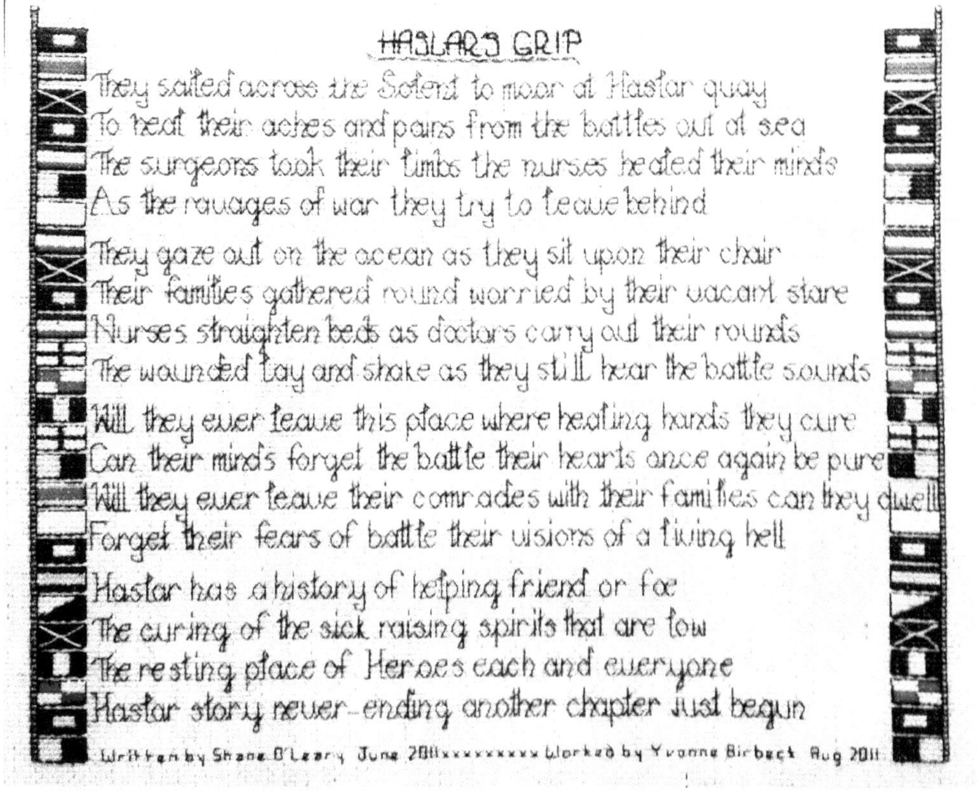

Written by Shane O'Leary of Harcourt Development, the company that works with the new owners, Haslar Developments Ltd, while on his first visit in 2011 and presented to Haslar Heritage Group. The late Yvonne Birbeck worked it in cross-stitch with the naval flag signal 'England Expects' and it now hangs in St Luke's Church.

A recruitment photograph for QARNNS and the Navy in the 1960s. In the background are the Nurses' Quarters and the Rose Garden, no longer in existence

CHAPTER TWO
'CARRY ON CARING' – STORIES FROM THE STAFF

When Haslar first opened, most of its staff were untrained, save for the physicians and even they had to pay for their education and supply their own instruments. In the beginning the nursing staff consisted mainly of widows and perhaps ladies of easy virtue: they only earned £1 a month and only then if they attended for work.

With as many as 1,800 patients at any time in the early years, the then civilian staff numbered in their hundreds and were employed in a vast range of roles from Block Matron, laundrywoman and, seamstress, to Agent, secretarial staff, pharmacists, butchers, plumbers and labourers – even people employed to scrape the sewer walls on a weekly basis.

Through the decades, staff increased in line with demand and on one occasion in the late eighteenth century 200 ladies were recruited through the Salisbury newspaper to work at Haslar as nurses, with Greenwich Pensioners also being employed in the nineteenth century.

By 1884, the Naval Nursing Service was formed (later to become Queen Alexandra's Royal Navy Nursing Service) and the Royal Naval Sick Berth branch came to Haslar, improving the care given to the patients of the day. Planned and organised training and examinations was the order of the day and by the time of the Great War, Haslar was a main training base for medical staff called up for service, along with RN Hospital Stonehouse in Plymouth.

During World War II, VAD (Voluntary Aid Detachment) nurses were also serving in Haslar alongside the QARNNS and Sick Berth Attendants. It was a demanding time with an influx of the injured from Dunkirk to D Day, during which Haslar dealt with thousands of the injured from the Normandy beaches.

Medical staff training was to continue at the Haslar Staff School until well into the 1990s and through specialist clinical training services within the military and NHS.

QARNNS nursing staff are fondly remembered: their crisp aprons and nursing caps, together with the triangular veils and uniform of the nursing sisters, all quickened the heart of many a male patient.

As in the 'Carry On' films, there was a side to the staff at Haslar that – as you'll read in this chapter – was romantic and funny. Many staff remember these stories, which were often retold at staff reunions.

Dead Man's Mile

When I went to Haslar for my induction I was lost for words: it was grand, to say the least. I walked through the main gates and then through the Arcade leading to the courtyard in the rear, with the ward and living buildings to the right and left, and a lovely church at the bottom with a lovely park of trees and flowers. It was indeed magnificent. I signed up five years.

Having joined up, I used to go shopping in Gosport and get the number 11 bus back to Haslar, asking the driver for the fare to Dead Man's Mile. It was named this because in the early 1800s when men were sick and taken off the sailing boats, their hammocks served as stretchers. They were lowered into rowing boats, rowed from the sea up Haslar creek under Pneumonia Bridge for about a mile, taken ashore at this point and brought along the road carried by two seamen and taken into Haslar. They had no water or dressings so most of them were dead by the time they got there, hence the name Dead Man's Mile.

Pneumonia Bridge was quite a steep bridge, open to all the elements. I remember taking two patients on afternoon leave, one with an arm in a cast and the other in a wheelchair, over the bridge to the pub called The Haslar Tavern on the other side. When we came back the tide was well out and we were a bit worse for wear. Somehow I lost control of the wheelchair and it carried on down the steep bridge. I was shouting "lean to the left!" but it went off the end and fell in the mud. The patient was fine; I managed to get him sorted and we decided not to say anything to anyone, but back on the ward they wanted to know where all the seaweed and mud had come from. My leave was stopped for a week.

As junior nurses not yet qualified we had to sign in and out; how far you were into your training depended on the time you had to sign in. I was into my second year and had to be in by 10pm, but I got persuaded to go to a party, after being in the Haslar pub. It was about 11.30pm when I came back. I had to climb a huge oak staircase where the quarters' sister was on duty. With a stern face she said:

"Drunk again, nurse."

I replied: "So am I."

The next day I was told what I had said but I couldn't remember it. My leave was stopped again. {I didn't get home much}. I used to put my good conduct badge on with Velcro because it was always coming off!

When I was working on receiving room {A&E} an important American officer – or so I thought – came into the department. I put him into the officers' room. I could hear the surgeon asking who had put him in that room. I said it was me and he asked why. I told him he was an officer off the aircraft carrier. He wasn't happy: it turned out the man was the vending machine repairer on the ship. I replied that he had all the stripes and stars, but it turned out they got them for every time they crossed the Atlantic.

Lynn Allison

The name Dead Man's Mile also had its origins in the time when, after 1859 when the Naval Cemetery was opened, funerals would leave Haslar by a large side gate into the mile. But the band was not permitted to play the funeral marches until the cortege turned from the mile and into Clayhall Road.

Pneumonia Bridge

Haslar paved the way for true love

It was 23 February 1981 and the members of Blaine Class (every class was given a name often associated with a famous Haslar name) who had arrived just a few weeks before to start their training, were already seasoned veterans of the Haslar Club. But tonight was something special: Z Class, a newly arrived batch of pretty young Naval Nurses, had arrived that day and it would only be polite to welcome them and give them the benefit of our wisdom in the ways of Nobby behind the bar (RIP) and how we would be extraordinarily pleased to show them all the local haunts over the coming months. As a branch transfer (if approved, one can transfer from, say, being a cook to being a Medical Assistant or vice versa), I had the benefit of being more than two years ahead of my compatriots in the Royal Navy, so was entirely confident I would be the one to whom the young ladies would all flock for such a guided tour.

Each member of Z Class had a unique beauty in her own way but I clearly remember one in particular who stood out from the rest. Lorraine was built like an X-Ray with clothes on and blessed with the longest blonde hair I'd ever seen: I was somewhat dismayed to discover that she was the daughter of a serving Chief Petty Officer Medical Assistant. Clearly this would pose a problem for me as he had the benefit of many more years' experience under his belt than me and would surely have warned his daughter about the ways of the sailor. Besides I didn't fancy my chances going forward in the branch if I upset her dad!

I was also hampered by the fact that I was skinny as a rake with enough facial hair to provide luxury accommodation for a family of field mice. I was later to discover that this would have been a bar to dating her anyway as apparently she didn't care for facial hair, whereas my younger classmates who'd just come from HMS *Raleigh*, were clean-shaven and super fit. Quite a few were budding Royal Marine Commando medics so it slowly dawned on me that perhaps this was one conquest that was not meant to be.

Time went by and one by one most of us ended up dating and taking the girls on the promised guided tours of the local area. But my thoughts were never far away from those golden locks. I was asked by her classmates to make a cake for her 21st birthday, which I duly arranged with the galley and decorated in my small cabin in Albert Block.

By 1982, Z Class was all out on various secondments and staying at HMS *Nelson*. They couldn't take their cuddly toys with them and had to vacate their cabins at Haslar, so they all struggled to find storage space. Being the gallant gentleman I was (and still trying to make an impression) I offered to store them in my cabin pending their return. They all arrived with black gash sacks full of the things! In total I think there were 100 or so stuffed cuddly toys, which made my small cabin even more strapped for space. However, little was I to know just how much trouble this gesture of gallantry was to cause. That year saw the Falklands conflict and I was among many dispatched to the South Atlantic under various commands to spank the bottoms of the Argentinians. It was not until I came back that I discovered that – working on the theory that we may not return – the Master at Arms had ordered the emptying of our cabins and all our kit had been placed into storage. Upon my return I had to explain why a seasoned sailor had so many soft cuddly toys in his cabin. I also had to explain why I had my own still and home-brew kit bubbling away in my locker, but that is the subject of a different story.

Not long after my return, I married one of the ladies of Z Class and we had two fantastic children.

Years later I came to realise that, deep down, my thoughts were still about that stunning blonde and the torch I always held for her. Lorraine had eventually married as well and as couples we went on our separate lives, though we all socialised at every opportunity. This was, for me, harder than it appeared on the surface. Our paths took very different routes and life did not always go smoothly. After leaving the QARNNS, she went on to become a successful businesswoman, before eventually returning to nursing many years later. Quite by chance, her husband contacted me to ask for some advice and it was only then that I discovered that they had been divorced for some years. My marriage had broken down too, but I never regretted the decision to get married and am very proud of my children.

Thanks to the development of social media I regained contact with her in early 2014 and we met up for the first time in over 22 years in the April. Thankfully, and after 38 years, she now approves of facial hair … and we will marry on 23 February 2019. We now have four wonderful children and two grandchildren between us.

When we first discussed the wedding we faced a few obstacles. She wanted to get married in St Luke's but that had closed years ago. The church, though still standing, no longer had a license to perform weddings – neither it didn't have any clergy. Besides, we were both divorced and Lorraine was a Catholic. Haslar holds so many memories for us both and it was really the only place we wanted to hold the ceremony. Negotiations with the various registrars in Devon (where we were living) and Hampshire enabled the publication of our banns to be done in Devon and the legal parts of the marriage ceremony completed in Fareham. Thanks to the chairman and trustees of the Haslar Heritage Group the church (which reopened for services in 2010) is being made available to us for a blessing service that will be conducted by two amazing people – Bishop Paul and Father Brizz (two gentlemen that I have had the honour and privilege of knowing for many years).

Haslar holds many memories for all who served there, but for us it will be like coming home; and I cannot thank the trustees of the Haslar Heritage Group enough for their help in making an old fella's dream come true.

Rod Newman

All those parquet floors!

I joined the QARNNS in April 1964 and stayed at Haslar until December 1965. I was in Principal Training School number 6 in September 1964 and graduated at RNH Stonehouse in October 1967.

I remember arriving at the front gate of Haslar to see this magnificent building, and all the beautiful grounds. We went to Training Division each morning at HMS *Dolphin*, with all the sailors yelling and whistling at us. Saturdays were cleaning days on Saturdays with Wardmaster Lt John Hammond doing inspections afterwards. They were large wards, typical of most hospitals at that time, but all those parquet floors to clean and polish! The lads did most of the heavy work and we got to clean up the sluice rooms. I remember using Cardinal polish to clean our red tile window sills.

Another thing they did was to send us to pick up our surgical patients. We were armed with a kidney basin containing a mouth gag (used to open patients' mouths when they vomited from anaesthetic) to help recovering patients.. I never needed to use it, thank God!

I also remember taking patients from the Orthopaedic wards outside in their beds during the summer months on sunny days to get some fresh air. I also worked working on the Zymotics wards on night shift that was the ward for infectious diseases. It was an eerie place; we had to keep a little fire going in the office and go outside for the coal. On the day shift there, we also had to wash up the dishes from meals for the TB patients.

We had lovely days going for a swim off the sea wall and walking to Stokes Bay.

I lived in G block for most of my time there – I moved cabin twice and ended up in a two-bed cabin with a classmate.

My last day was a sad one. My trunk had been packed for Malta and I only had a suitcase and kit bag left to take with me. I knew deep down I would not be returning there.

They were happy times. I returned in 2002 with another QARNNS friend, and was disappointed to see that the wall facing the sea had gone. Replaced with fencing, it looked weird.

Rita Rideout (née Higgins)

The 'things' in the jars

My mum was a cleaner at Haslar in the early 1970s. She used to clean in the medical museum, which was locked and out of bounds to the public. I remember when it was the school holidays she used to take me along – I must have only been about five or six. I was never allowed inside and had to sit outside and wait until she had finished. She hated cleaning in there and said she never looked up at the 'things' that were kept in the jars.

Marilyn Paternotte

How do you plead?

In 1973, I was up on Captain's table for being absent without leave, a serious offence in the Royal Navy.

"Right," said the Petty Officer Medical Assistant. "You know the drill. You march in, stand in front of the Captain's table, salute, off cap, and stand at ease."

"Right – I know the drill, PO."

"Aright, Paddy, relax – you have a few minutes to spare."

The order came, I did the drill and stood at ease in front of the Senior Medical Officer. The charge was read out:

"Absent without leave. MA Franklin, how do you plead?"

"Guilty, sir," I replied, in my strong Irish accent.

"Tell us why you went AWOL, Franklin."

"Well sir …" I started talking really fast in my Irish accent.

"Stop," said the Captain. "I cannot understand a word you are saying. Slow down and take your time."

"Yes sir," I replied. I started again to speak and again the Senior Medical Officer could not understand what I was saying. This time he spoke to my Petty Officer Medical Assistant.

"Is their anyone else from Ireland that can understand him?"

"There is," said the Petty Officer. "Medical Assistant Muldowney."

"Go and get him."

So they found Muldowney pretty quick and in he came, and they explained to him what was needed.

I started again and this time MA Muldowney repeated every word I said clearly.

"You're Irish too, Muldowney?" asked the SMO.

"No sir. I was born and raised in London."

For all of Muldowney translation, I didn't do much good. The SMO sentenced me to twenty-eight days in Royal Naval Detention Quarters, but it was probably the first time that an interpreter had been used to translate what another English-speaking person was saying.

Richard Franklin

Fetch me my Rolls Royce

I was working as a Leading Medical Assistant on A3 officers' ward. On this particular morning I answered my cabin bell to be met by a voice that said: "Ah steward, can you get my car for me?"

"Whereabouts is it, sir?"

"In the garage," he replied.

I went off and made a phone call to the garage, and sure enough they had the car, which they duly delivered to the front of 'A' block and I took delivery of the keys on the ward.

I informed the officer that his car was below, to which he replied: "Take me to it – my case is there. I'm being discharged this morning."

I did as instructed and handed over the keys that belonged to a blue Rolls Royce which had a signalman mascot on the bonnet.

You may have guessed the owner: Lord Mountbatten. I saluted as he drove off – this was around 9am.

Later that morning, around 11am, the Surgeon Rear Admiral and his entourage arrived on the ward to say their farewells and asking his whereabouts.

"Why did you let him go?" I was in deep water once again!

Douglas Cramp

A smile and a shiver

I was working on C5 ward, which at the time was 'dirty surgery' (the term for surgery that dealt with patients who had abscesses, or had rectal surgery). The patient's dressings were part of the morning and afternoon ritual, not the most pleasant of tasks for patient, or nurse. I spotted a Medical Assistant (he shall remain nameless) walking down the ward with a bottle in his hand.

"Where are you going with that?' I asked him.

"Off to do a Lysol dressing."

"It's called Eusol, ya moron. Do a dressing using that stuff and the patient would learn to fly."

He was banned from doing dressings, but it was the casual ease with which he sauntered towards the dressing room that still brings me a smile and a shiver.

Peter Simpson

Eusol stands for Edinburgh University Solution of Lime. Lysol is a disinfectant.

The 'horrible hand'

I was on night duty for the second week on F6 (Orthopaedics). The first week we had been a bit busy and not got up to any stunts, but now it was the penultimate night so we thought we would do the 'horrible hand'. That was an examination glove filled with lukewarm water, dragged across the back of a nurse's neck. It feels awful! We thought we'd add some blue dye because it was the wrong colour. Then, just like Frankenstein's monster, the stunt grew into a six-foot dummy that pumped real blood. We dressed it in my clothes, as I lived ashore. My partner-in-crime had made a head and drawn some eyes that seemed to follow you.

We placed it in the treatment room and called the duty sister. We told her we had a road accident case and it looked as if there was an arterial bleed. She came running and saw blood pumping through the dressing ... we really had her going for a couple of minutes before she realised.

Sister thought it was great and called the nurse from F3, who promptly fainted on seeing the blood pumping out. Excellent! Sister then called her colleague from the other side of the hospital, who asked where the Principal Medical Officer was. She told him he was tied up with the other casualties, his deputy too, so sister came running – cape flying – from the other side of the hospital. All gathered around the 'casualty'.

"Are his feet cold?" she asked.

"I don't know," we said, handing her one.

Another time I was on nights on 'dirty surgery', which was next to the children's ward. I heard a baby crying: it was completely inconsolable. It cried and cried, an angry/hurt cry. At dinner I saw the nurse – a friend of mine – who was on the ward and said she'd obviously had a tough night with the baby. She replied that there were no babies on the ward.

Talking to a children's nurse later, I described the crying: she told me that was one of the symptoms of a brain irritation and that, a long time ago, a baby had died on the ward from that disease.

Alan Herbert

Freeze-bottles at the ready!

In early 1966 I visited Haslar as a schoolboy. Along with six other young lads, I was shown around the hospital by a Wardmaster, Lieutenant John Hammond, who finished the tour in the hospital's medical museum. Here for the first time I saw dissected bodies in large glass jars, unborn Siamese twins, and a full-size skeleton complete with all the arteries and veins still connected. Afterwards we were taken to the staff canteen and offered beef burgers in buns with tomato sauce. Needless to say I stuck to just the tea and biscuits, not having the stomach for anything else. I wasn't, however, put off the Medical Branch as I joined a year later.

I formally joined Haslar in 1968 and began training on F6 Ward (male genito-urinary). Fellow staff consisted of a Leading Hand (five foot four with a Hitler ego), an overweight Medical Assistant who could just about push a tea trolley, another Medical Assistant who was only interested in showing staff and patients magic card tricks and a Chief Medical Technician who only ever appeared early each morning during treatment time, when he would proceed to shove various sized knitting needles up the penises of poor sailors who were suffering from urinary retention. It used to make my eyes water constantly.

Every weekend was devoted to carrying out urine testing, which in those days meant using numerous tablets on small pieces of blotting paper, putting a few drops of urine on top and noting if the paper changed colour. We used to test for everything from protein and acetone to blood. On one morning I was very flustered, having upwards of 100 different tests to do assisted by a junior nurse. She kept asking me very stupid questions, which began to annoy me. At one point she asked for the umpteenth time how to test for sugar. I told her to dip her finger in and taste it – and yes, she did.

Tuesdays was operation day, often with just circumcisions being carried out. Upwards of ten sailors would arrive back in the ward minus a useless piece of skin with numerous stitches in place. Beside each bed we would place ethyl chloride sprays (freeze bottles) for the lads to use should they get an unfortunate erection.

At the time we had a very good-looking staff nurse who, like other nurses, wore black stockings under her ward dress. She would occasionally walk down the ward and bend over on the pretext of picking up some fallen document or item of clothing. Within minutes there would be a sudden whooshing sound from all the sprays being activated.

Periodically we were required to do two weeks of night duty. In those days any abdominal area operations required a nipples-to-knees shave using a cut-throat razor. Shaving around the more sensitive areas required great skill and dexterity. One slip and the operation was probably no longer required. One evening I was asked to shave a woman who was having an emergency appendectomy. The shave was no problem but it did make me smile when I saw her two tattooed lanterns swinging from each nipple with the words 'Port' and 'Starboard'.

On another ward we had two patients, one with a serious heart condition who was not expected to live, and the other – a chap called Foote – who had a mild prostate problem and was due to be discharged in a few days' time. He was a very likeable chap with whom I often had interesting chats. One morning I entered the ward and said my normal "Good morning, Mr Foote." He didn't reply but just stared at me. I quickly realised that he wasn't breathing and shouted out "cardiac arrest!" to my colleagues. We

Above: Clinical Measurements staff.
Below: All change! QARNNS Nurses and Nursing Sisters mark the demise of the original uniform in 2008

all attempted to bring him back with heart massage, but after thirty minutes the Medical Officer declared Mr Foote dead.

Later in the staffroom, when I was feeling very upset, the MO asked me what was wrong. I said that I was sad at the unexpected death and more importantly what was he going to say to Mr Foote's wife, who was due to visit? The MO looked at me and said: "I shall tell her that sadly she has one foot in the grave already." I smiled at this and the MO said I should never get too attached to my patients, as situations like this would make me very depressed. His advice was always to remain detached, but I was never sure if he was right.

When someone died on a ward, the staff would wrap the body in a white sheet and place it in a bier (a kind of metal boxed trolley). The bier was then wheeled outside the main hospital building and over to the Pathology Department, where the Mortuary was housed. One Christmas night when it was heavily snowing, all the trainees were called out from their beds and told to form into search parties. A bier had arrived at the Mortuary minus the body. It had fallen out somewhere in the snow and the porters couldn't find it. We were out there for two hours in the freezing cold looking for it before someone found it under a bush where it had rolled.

Having qualified as a Medical Assistant, I – like other newly qualified MAs – was lined up outside the Regulating Office where the Master at Arms would tell us what our next draft would be, all of us desperately wanting a ship in order to 'see the world'. As each lad left the office we would ask: "Have you got a ship?" Dejectedly he would reply: "No. I got a bloody shore establishment." I was the last lad in and I was told I had HMS *Belfast*. I asked if it was a ship and was told it was. I proudly told the lads waiting outside that I had got a ship and went merrily back to the ward. The Medical Officer in charge asked what draft I'd got.

"A ship, sir. HMS Belfast," I replied smugly.

He burst out laughing.

"Is it a genuine ship, sir?"

"Oh yes, in fact it is currently moored in Portsmouth Harbour."

"Why did you laugh, then?"

"HMS Belfast is an old decommissioned battleship," he said. "It's used as the HQ for the reserve fleet also moored in Portsmouth Harbour. It will never go to sea again but might well end up going to the scrapyard."

To say I was upset would be an understatement. Fortunately I only served on Belfast for a matter of weeks before I got a new draft to HMS *Victory Barracks* – a shore establishment!

I returned to Haslar many years later as a Petty Officer and in later years as a Lieutenant RN (Medical Services). I always felt it a great honour and privilege to have served at such an historic hospital with such skilled and wonderful people.

Michael Raven

I know that tattoo!

In the mid-1970s I was an ambulance man working out of the Eastern Road station in Portsmouth. On one occasion my crew-mate and I had to take a patient to Haslar Hospital for an appointment and we were told to wait for the patient and return them home.

We were offered the chance to have a look around the small museum at the hospital. Apart from some rather grisly human remains of a sailor who died in Freetown, Sierra Leone, I noticed a display of photographs of the various tattoos sailors had inflicted upon themselves.

One that made me cringe was of a fly tattooed on the end of a very sensitive part of his anatomy. Another one I recognised immediately was of Popeye the Sailorman. His legs were emblazoned on the front of each thigh and his mouth was the man's navel. The middle part I will leave to your imagination.

Having previously served in the Royal Navy, at one time on HMS *Hermione*, I recognised the tattoo as one my messmate had, a very outgoing and funny man. Someone had found it worthy to photograph him in the nude.

Bill Swinfield

A commando encounter

I was the seamstress at Haslar for over 25 years. I have many 'sewing room' memories, but one I will never forget concerned a chap who came in because he had torn his trousers. He was very chatty and as I waited for him to take off his trousers he told me he was going in the commandos.

"Wow, that's great," I said enthusiastically, but on turning round I realised he wasn't 'going in' in the commandos ... he was GOING commando!

He never batted an eyelid and neither did I till he left the room, when I came over all unnecessary!

June Chambers

Dr Souter was gorgeous!

I worked at Haslar in the early 1970s as a civvie receptionist in the X-ray department and it was the best job I ever had. I was working at Camper & Nicholsons at the time I went for my interview. This was in the days that you could pick and choose your jobs. I was interviewed by a lovely, gruff man called Mr Gutteridge. He told me what the wage was and I told him I was already paid more at Camper's, which was a fib! We then bartered until I got what I wanted, so I gave my notice in at Camper's and joined Haslar. I was about 18 or 19 years old.

Every Monday morning we used to get a lot of Navy divers coming over from HMS *Dolphin*, to have chest X-rays before going through the tank. When I was 20, the love of my life came in for an X-ray. We talked and he asked if I was going to the weekly dance at Vernon, so my friend and I went over to it. He was there, but he was leaving the Navy and was going to Singapore for 10 days as his last job.

By the time he came back and out in to civvie street, I was packed and ready and we moved to Edinburgh! He was doing saturation diving for a company called Comex, off the oil rigs, working three weeks on and one week off. I got a job in the tax offices just outside Edinburgh, then we moved to Portugal, with him still working. Civil War broke out and we had to come home. He brought me back to my mum and dad's while he went to Stockport to look for somewhere for us to live and I never saw him again! I was heartbroken and have never forgotten him.

Every month at Haslar, the Chief's Mess used to have what they called a 'Bring and Buy'. Basically, it was a delicious buffet and free drinks. Our Chief, whose name was Whitfield, always used to take us office staff over to them and we'd have a great afternoon. The two other ladies – Pat and Mollie – worked for Dr Souter, who was gorgeous. All the Naval medical staff were lovely to work for; I really missed them when I left and still think of them.

Chief Whitfield was a Geordie who liked his tea so strong that you could stand a spoon up in it. There was a short-tempered Irish Chief called Finnebar O'Neill, a Welsh lad called Lyn and a few others whose names I can't remember. I went out with a few of the staff from there, one in particular called Jed. Many years later, when my son was at The Royal Hospital School, I bumped into Jed, who also had a son there. It was good to catch up. He was just about to take up a new job in Northamptonshire. By coincidence, this is where I live now. We did make arrangements to meet, as by then we were both divorced, but I got cold feet at the last minute!

Karen Harrop

My face was as red as my belt

I began my nursing training at Haslar in September 1965. I had just turned 18 and recently graduated from an all-girls school. I was so naive! I think my face was often as red as my first year belt. New nurses were teased lot but it was all in good humour.

I was drafted to Malta for a year and spent four months working in the sick bay at RNAS Arbroath, giving me experiences that none of my friends training in civvy street had.

The hours were long, conditions tough and almost archaic by today's standards, but patients recovered and were sent back to duty. In those days, Britain had a Navy worldwide!

I had wanted to be a nurse since the age of seven. When my aunt began her training at a London hospital, she stayed with my family on days off and the tales of her experiences entertained us.

I joined the QAs quite by chance: a school friend was applying to the Wrens and in her package was a brochure about the QAs. The chance to travel while training appealed to me: I applied and was accepted. My friend served for six years – our paths never crossed in duty but we remain friends to this day.

Gill Grove (née Hicks)

Foreman of labour

A book about Haslar would not be complete without mention of Bill Gutteridge. He was Foreman of Labour for many years and all the workers were under him. He was in charge of the cleaning, the gardens and of clocking in and out. He did that until he retired, then the same job was done by many people.

I was employed as a woodwork instructor and when I turned up to start I found the job did not exist. So I started it and it became a large department, which ended up being an occupational therapy department for patients. In 1980 I got the MBE for my work there.

Ron Cross

The woodworking Occupational Therapy department

It was a miracle

I am writing this on behalf of Haslar Intensive Care and Hyperbaric Unit staff and especially a young male patient from Switzerland who I shall refer to as David. In 1995 Haslar had opened a new Hyperbaric Unit with a specialist six-man chamber complete with patient support and ventilator to support the breathing of the unconscious patient. As Anaesthetic Technical Officer, helping with the refurbishment of the Unit, I was there when David arrived.

He arrived one evening with a police escort from London's Canary Wharf, unconscious and suffering from carbon monoxide poisoning. He had moved to a new apartment, gone to bed and been found unconscious: the cause was eventually identified as a blocked flue in the apartment's boiler.

David was transferred to the Hyperbaric Unit and was ventilated in the main chamber: this continued on a regular basis for a few days and he was nursed on the Intensive Care Unit. One of the team who looked after him was Leading Naval Nurse Alison Hofman (now Captain Hofman, Defence Nursing Advisor).

At that time the ICU was being moved to D5 ward (the old A5) where a temporary unit had been put in place. The move went well and treatment continued, but sadly with little signs of improvement. The Consultants had various discussions and decided to ventilate David using a nitric oxide mixture. The gas was delivered in a pink cylinder from Southampton General, where it was used in Paediatrics. In setting this up in the temporary ICU, we had to vent the expired gas – this was done by passing a tube from the patient out through the window. The tube was quite a length and dropped below the external floor level of D5.

A day or so later we discovered that the end of the tube was hanging directly in line with the open window of the Matron's Office – oops! We quickly ran back inside and pulled the tube in by a few feet.

Slowly David responded to the treatment and Matron was none the wiser as to her brush with expired nitric oxide! (In fact in 1998 nitric oxide was classed as the 'Molecule of the Year' and was in found to be useful in cardiovascular treatment).

Eventually David made a full recovery and the ICU moved back into a brand new state-of-the-art facility; one of the most up-to-date in Southern England. David left Haslar and went back to Switzerland and his family, who had spent weeks patiently by his bedside.

Some months later the doors of the Unit opened and there stood David with the largest bar of Toblerone on his shoulder. From that day he returned on a number of occasions and became great friends with the ICU and Hyperbaric staff, with many a supper taken in the local area, Toblerone eaten and time spent chatting and getting to know David and his family very well.

The visits faded, but that was some 22 years ago now. David – and what was seen as a miracle at the time – is still greatly remembered.

Eric Birbeck

How did the film end?

How things have changed since 1962! Can you imagine nurses having to be in by 10.30pm? It often meant leaving the Ritz cinema before the end of the film. Miss Beasley would be on patrol to make sure you were in, with dear old VAD Nurse Heatherington sneaking you up the back stairs if you should dare to be a few minutes late.

I remember being issued with sanitary towels that were so large, but fabulous for cleaning your rooms … kit musters, chasing around the corridors to borrow items of clothing that you had disposed of … and being one of the first nurses to go to the cenotaph, having spent weeks at HMS *Excellent* learning how to march (we had to jump over puddles rather than march through them). How proud we were when we got there:

recall my parents' disgust when they watched it on television and Richard Dimbleby didn't know who we were, following the Wrens.

Jacqui Brooks (née Jones)

Not another body, surely?

A small storage building was being constructed on the south side of the hospital and in the absence of the Commander I was informed that a skeleton had been found while digging the foundations. This was not in an area of the grounds where there were supposed to have been burials. We were not sure how old the body was and there was nothing in the regulations that covered this, so we called the MOD Police. It must have been a slow day for them because they called in a Hampshire Constabulary forensic team and we had police lines established, screens erected and all sorts of police on the scene. It was established fairly quickly that the skeleton was from the days of Trafalgar and the police disappeared as quickly as they came! We then had the issue of what to do with the body. The Medical Officer in Charge decided that this poor soul had to have a ceremonial burial, so a guard of honour was arranged with a bugler.

After the burial, we settled back into our regular lives until a few days later I was asked to go over to the building site to discuss the finding of another body. This time the MOD Police came over, took one look and said: "yes, this is another one."

"What about forensics?" we asked.

"No," they said. "He just needs reburying like the last one."

Well this time we did it without the guard of honour and as a bugler was not available we got someone who played the instrument very badly to come over and stumble their way through The Last Post.

A day later we found another body – this time no MOD Police but straight to reburial with no guard and no bugler, just a priest saying a prayer of two.

In the end we had five or six bodies and the historians at the hospital suggested that what might have happened was due to the fact that when someone died at night in the hospital the nurses had to fill in the various papers. If you took the body out and buried it in the grounds you could avoid the paperwork, so that might be why they were buried in unmarked graves.

Glenn Duggan

A word with the Princess

I did a school work-placement in 1991-19922 in the X-ray department when I was 15. It happened to have coincided with a visit from Her Royal Highness Princess Alexandra. She came over to me. I was quite far back but she moved people aside to speak to me and asked what I was doing there. When I explained I wanted to be a nurse and was doing a work-placement via school, she was very interested.

Ten years later I worked at Haslar in the dermatology department as a qualified nurse.

Rachel Daly

Dressed for the ball

My first impression of Haslar when I attended for interview as a 17-year-old was of sandbags round a sentry point and someone with a gun. This was at the height of the First Gulf War and it made a far-off conflict suddenly feel very real. During the next two days I fell in love with the hospital.

After basic training we moved into Medical Branch Staff Quarters, which was a warren of a building with big rooms for four to share and small TV rooms. There was even a small galley where we would make piles of toast to keep us going as we studied or, more often, as a way of procrastinating when we were meant to be studying.

On the wards themselves, there were long rows of beds down each side of the Nightingale wards. Each bed had matching blue blankets and nearly every patient was out of bed. The floors were always shiny from buffing. Eighteen months into our training we earned our buckles to wear on our belts. Night shifts were seven on and seven off and then there were the queues to collect leave passes on the Monday morning, everyone giggly with tiredness. We worked hard on the wards caring for the local population as well as service personnel and veterans from around the country.

The church played a large part in the hospital, for funerals, weddings and Sunday services. I was confirmed there by the Bishop of the forces, a special occasion that my parents came to on a sunny day. There was also a music group that I belonged to that met one evening a week in the church. We mostly played wind instruments and enjoyed a variety of music and an escape from the pressures of the wards. One lovely summer evening we had left the door open and a fox walked up the aisle and sat down in front of the altar washing itself as we played.

Every year we would dress up in ball gowns and smart suits for the junior rates summer ball. Even the patients would get involved, wanting to hear descriptions of what people were going to wear. We even went up to the wards before the ball to show our dresses sometimes.

One Christmas was particularly special. My then boyfriend completed a night shift in the labs where he was an RAF Corporal. We enjoyed a Christmas dinner together, which he cooked on the tiny stove in Canada block, and then he proposed to me before I went off to do my afternoon shift on the ward. I couldn't stop grinning all afternoon.

The togetherness and warmth of the hospital is the greatest memory I have. The whole hospital knew each other. We knew who was where and if you didn't know the answer to something you would know someone who did. I trained and served at Haslar from 1992-1999.

Sarah Wilde

Fox came to take a look

I worked at Haslar in my early 20s as part of the admin team. I remember typing up lunch menus on an old typewriter, with a fox coming into the office for a casual look in our bin ...

I was a clerical officer, doing patient records and I saw the whole medical museum, even the underground one with its medical samples from the whole history of the Navy.

The place did play a big role in my life: my brother and I were Navy kids, so we both got to go to Haslar's A&E for a couple of things. When I was a kid, I was in the Dolphin Cadets. I literally grew up in a Naval environment, and even when I had a summer job at 16 it was as a cleaner round HMS *Dolphin*, including the submarine museum.

I worked at Haslar in civil admin for about two years for the MOD, then went back after maternity leave and worked for the private contractor that took over the wardroom mess catering contract.

Caroline Lee

Who spiked the sugar?

While working on B5 – the Orthopaedic ward – in the 1960s I was asked by a young Surgeon Lieutenant to make coffee for all the Consultants who had just come out of theatre and taken up residence in the Sister's office – I think it was Sister Turtle.

This I duly did, taking in trays of coffee and a bowl of sugar. A couple of minutes later the said Surgeon Lt came tearing down the ward and grabbed me by the ear, frog marching me into the office.

"Drink that!" he said.

I tasted the coffee, which was very salty to say the least. Once again I was in trouble. To this day I do not know who doctored the sugar. I suspect some disgruntled patient thought it would be a joke at my expense.

I was never asked to make coffee for them again.

I was, it seemed, accident-prone; walking down the ward with a tray of medicine glasses containing gargles for tonsillectomy patients on F3 ward, I slipped and landed on my backside. Of course not one glass survived. The tirade of language coming from the Sister (who shall remain nameless) was less than ladylike. At the time I think I was one of youngest qualified Sick Berth Attendants, being only 17 years old (I had been an HMS *Ganges* boy).

On the same ward I was on nights on my own and was questioned by the duty Wardmaster, John Hammond, about being on night duty especially on my own, due to my young age. Great, I thought – that's the end of doing nights. No such luck!

Douglas Cramp

Dad was 'Head Turncock'

My father Ted Churcher started work at Haslar in 1975. He was 'Head Turncock', now known as a plumber. Because he was a key worker he was given no. 5 Haslar cottages to live in with my mum, me and my brother and sister. We have happy memories of living there.

My dad was diagnosed with cancer in 1980 and died in 1981; my mum remained living at Haslar for some years until it got too much for her as it was a three-storey house. We'd all moved out and she couldn't manage it on her own anymore.

I have so many memories of Haslar: my uncle Ron Barnes also worked there as a barber for many years until he retired.

Cheryl Rolls (née Churcher)

Above: Hospital staff bound for Portsmouth on the Haslar ferry with HM Submarine Grampus in the background
Below: Recruiting and prospective Nurses being given a tour of Haslar prior to interview

The Toothwright's tale

In 1964 a Dental Clinic was already well established in a fine location on the first floor of the main front block of the Hospital, more or less above the Main Arcade. The surgeries looked northeastwards directly down on to the original and at that time only, Main Gate.

1964 was still very much the era of 'upright' chairside dentistry and any dental officer waiting in that clinic for an impression to set would easily observe a pair of straight iron rails set into the small road below him, leading away down to the Haslar Jetty. RNH Haslar had been built to care for His Majesty's sick and injured seamen and traditionally these patients were landed at the jetty by boat from the Fleet at Spithead after which they were hauled into the hospital in wagons along these rails. But by 1964 this particular transport to Hospital Admissions was no longer in use! Nevertheless it was probable that the majority of walking patients and most hospital staff still arrived each day at the same jetty, having crossed from HM Dockyard or one of the naval establishments around the harbour by boat.

Of course there had always been land access to Haslar by road through Alverstoke or Gosport, but in the mid-1960s not many patients or staff owned a private car and those who came by road around the harbour had to face a journey of some 17 miles. On rare but memorable occasions, badly injured patients were brought from ships at sea by helicopter. The aircraft landed on the playing fields in HMS *Dolphin* adjacent to the main gate. Such evolutions were easily observed from the 1964 Dental Clinic.

There were two operating lists a week, one on a Monday morning and one on a Thursday afternoon. In the sixties there was something of a pattern to these operating lists. By the late 1970s, the dental health of the men in the Fleet had improved, underpinned by the newly introduced WRNS Dental Hygienists.

Rating inpatients were accommodated in wards near the Dental Department, but officer patients went to a separate Officers' Block, which was some two hundred yards away. They travelled to and from the operating theatre by 'tilly'. First to the Main Arcade and then by a rather ponderous lift which took them to the floors above.

This Officers' Block was closed after a few years and it was replaced by an Officers' Ward situated within the main hospital. It eventually became the School of Naval Medical Staff Training where, in 1987 Surgeon Captain S N Bussell, an Oral Surgery Consultant, became its Officer-in-Charge as the Director of Medical Staff Training.

Much later, when the Defence Secondary Care Agency became established in 1996 the old Officers' Block became the main administration block for the hospital's Commanding Officer's staff. At that time the newly named department of Oral and Maxillofacial Surgery moved into Haslar's old administration corridor in what had originally been 'A' block adjacent to the Main Arcade. Surgeon Captain John Holland appreciated the irony of sitting on the exact point from where distinguished Admirals and Medical Officers-in-Charge had run the whole Hospital for at least a century or more!

There was nothing unusual in departments moving around in Haslar. It had long been recognised that the modernisation of Haslar actually began as soon as the hospital was completed in 1762 … and it never really stopped afterwards. John Holland, a long time Haslar hand, used to observe that all the hospital departments, wards and offices instinctively tended to demonstrate a slow amoeba like movement. This ensured that if staff moved away for more than a month or two, they would need to undergo a period of reorientation upon return. It kept one on one's toes! At one time all the blocks were re-lettered to run alphabetically from the northwest corner so 'E' Block became 'A' Block and 'A' Block became 'D' Block etc. – chaos reigned!

Although the uniformed staff in the Dental Department changed every couple of years or so in typical naval fashion one stalwart civilian Mr Charles Milne MBE, provided extraordinary continuity in the Department from the 1950s, into the 1960s and on to the mid 1970s. He ran the office and managed the appointments, paperwork, reports and returns, the shipping of laboratory work and the ordering of stores. Nobody arrived in the clinic for duty before Mr Milne did, and nobody left later.

One summer afternoon a year Charlie Milne would leave his desk and go to the Hospital's annual Sports Day, which was held on the HMS *Dolphin* playing fields. There, every year right up to his retirement, he would invariably win the Veterans' 100 yard sprint! When he finally retired in 1975, Surgeon Captain Alec Smith arranged a suitable presentation to acknowledge Charlie Milne's 58 years of service to the Crown. He had completed 34 years with the Royal Marines and 24 years with the Dental Branch – surely something of a record.

Not only did the WRNS DSAs rapidly become efficient at surgical assisting, but several additionally came to master the mysteries of orthodontic chairside nursing, where there was an array of individual orthodontic brackets for every tooth and a bewildering range of different arch wires. By the 1990s, every orthodontic bracket and every arch wire used in the Straight Wire Technique had a different, sixteen-digit NATO stock number! No sooner had this orthodontic inventory been mastered, than the management of facial fractures delivered another array of complexity in the form of titanium plates with their special screws and special instruments.

Whenever 'drafty' insisted on moving a competent Wren DSA to another establishment, usually after eighteen months or two years in post, one's spirits would sink, but their replacements nearly always rose quickly up the steep learning curve and rapidly became as competent as their predecessors.

The WRNS Dental Senior Rates who organised everything, were often outstanding and worked hard integrating quickly not only into a new clinical environment but also mastering the strange, complex, hospital administration and record system and acquired an uncanny ability to find records misfiled by the resident staff.

RNDS Regulations did not normally entitle any retired personnel to primary dental care, but other regulations stated that Admirals of the Fleet remained on the 'Permanent List'! Thus, one day the Clinic in E Block was privileged to treat Admirals of the Fleet Earl Mountbatten of Burma and Lord Fraser of North Cape. At their request, they met together after their appointments for coffee in a cabin on the Officers' Ward, and the Medical Mess provided its best silver pot and china cups.

Timothy Hall

What's that noise?

Haslar grounds supported many foxes and one evening in the mid 1980s I was a member of the duty operating team. I was returning to the Crosslink operating theatres, having had supper. On entering the ground floor and starting up the stairs I heard a ruckus going on, including squeals from nurses. On investigation, three nurses had climbed onto an operating trolley and were being encircled by a lone fox. After the fox was driven off, it appeared that he had not been met by the usual staff with his supper, normally supplied by ward staff from left over scraps of patients' suppers.

After the Crosslink was built, two Portacabins were used as well on the lawn between the Crosslink and the main building, housing the Dermatology Department. In the early days a fox lived under the Portacabin. It was suffering from mange and was treated as private patient for a short while.

Eric Birbeck

A pair of Pusser's socks

I cannot remember what date in 1982 it was that Canberra docked in Southampton and I was reunited with my family, but three little memories have come back which showed the gulf between those of us who went down south and those who stayed behind.

As with everyone else in the Haslar Surgical Support Team I was given a month's well-earned leave to be with my family. When I got home there was a letter waiting for me from the 'Joss', the Master at Arms at Haslar, telling me to return to duty in half that time. No explanations!

When I returned to my desk in MACCO – the staff regulating (admin) office – with a face like thunder a certain Quarters Assistant said to me: "I don't know why you are looking so pissed off – we have been really busy here."

When I returned my kit to Stores I was missing a pair of pusser's green socks. The stores assistant started writing out a Stores Lost form for me. At this point my tolerance threshold had been exceeded. I told the PONTI (Person of No Tactical Importance) that unless he wanted to see a photo of the C126 on the front page of The Sun newspaper alongside his name, he should carefully reconsider his options – which he duly did.

I doubt if any of those three people were ever troubled by their actions, words or deeds, but I look back on it now with some sadness and amusement because my experience was rather trivial compared to those men who came back with bits missing from their bodies or minds. However, I am willing to bet those guys encountered the same mean, unthinking small-mindedness alongside the kindness and thoughtfulness of other more generous and thoughtful people.

Karl Rich

QARNNS Nurses at work and play

QARNNS members (left to right) Ron Duke, Gina Wilkinson, Russell Etherington, Sandra Snape, Joe O'Boyle, Gill McNaughton, Sarah Griffiths, Ros Ceaser-Scammel and Nick Casson

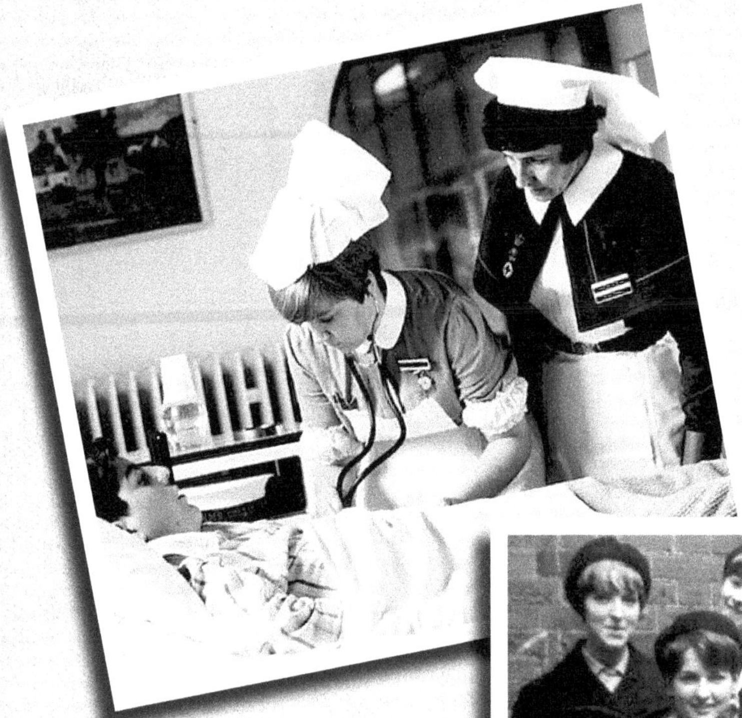

Top: A QARNNS Student Nurse working under the supervision of Senor Nursing Sister K Funnell. Centre: New joiner nurses. Bottom: QARNNS Medical Assistants pose in their ward and walking-out dress in 1989

Above: A class in training visits the hospital museum and library.
Below: Everyone who trained at Haslar will remember marching back and forth between Haslar and Training Division

Hanging up the clogs and scrubs

I started my nurse training back in 1970, as Probationary Registered Nurse Lesley Holmes. I started in Haslar with Sister Curtis, and I wonder where she and the rest of my PTS are now? They were happy times and the beginning of a nursing career that I have just retired from, having worked in operating theatres all my working life, and ending with voluntary work with the Mercy Ships organisation, which is the only NGO surgical hospital ship. It works mainly in West Africa giving free surgeries to anyone who has a need. I was with them short-term – a month every year for six years – then full time aboard for four-and-a-half years. Time to hang up my clogs and scrubs now!

Lesley Davey (née Holmes)

Big Ben sounds the alarm

When I think of the years I spent at Haslar, there are so many memories that I consider as special but are difficult to describe. I always loved that feeling of walking through the main gate and the archway, with every day holding fun or a unique memory or experience. I loved my nursing uniform and there was always a sense of pride putting it on. In the early years we shared dormitories and I can never remember arguments or bad feeling between occupants. However, I was not very popular when my Big Ben alarm was left on full sound in the Annexe one day and everyone ran out of their rooms thinking it was the fire alarm. But what delight when during the third year of our training we were allocated the luxury of single rooms.

During my 40 years of nursing there were times after leaving the QARNNS when I did not look forward to work, but I can honestly say I never had that feeling working at Haslar. The day-to-day memories are still very clear in my mind, for example giving proper bed baths, cleaning the metal bedpans in the sluice, racing into bed fully dressed before the Duty Nurse looked in to check you were in bed, walking over as a class in Number 1 uniforms to Training Division, swimming off the Haslar sea wall, catching up in the NAAFI before going on duty, slipping down to the galley at midnight to have a chat and make hot chocolate. The environment was calm, organised and protective and what I learnt and experienced at Haslar shaped my character, my views and ultimately my clinical practice through the rest of my career.

Hilary Butterworth

A Corporal Jones moment

With fond memories of Haslar, I am now a successful playwright writing mainly comedy. However, I feel I have failed in respect of the following two stories, in that I would dearly like to incorporate these in some comedy situation. But it just hasn't happened, so far. Perhaps I might have some moment of inspiration …

In the 60s I was in charge of 'M' Wards on the day a senior sister did a ward inspection. This senior sister, notorious for being somewhat pompous and always referring to junior staff by their surname, irrespective of rank or rating, arrived on the ward at the same time as a Sick Berth Attendant. He was one of the last conscripts, but one who showed his disrespect for seniority by not giving way to the good lady when they met on the stairwell. The senior sister wanted to know the SBA's surname, which he declined to give. The 'I want', became 'I demand' coupled with, "I have to know your surname." The SBA still refused, adding that she would not like it. When the sister persisted with a threat of reporting him for insubordination, he gave in. "Well, what is it?" she demanded.

The SBA smiled and said "Darling."

A second story concerns the very old and enormous extendable fire escape ladder that, when not in use, was housed in the base of the water tower. Occasionally it was wheeled out by junior SBAs for practice drill. I recall one occasion when it was set up by A Block and extended to the A3 Ward windows, its full extension.

"Any volunteers to go up?" asked the Petty Officer in charge. The lads took in the height and kept silent. "No?" asked the PO.

Then came a response, one that was very much like a Dad's Army Corporal Jones moment, as one of their number volunteered:

"Please sir, I'd like to be the one who goes up the ladder. I'm good at scaling ladders."

Our man was halfway up the ladder before the Petty Officer had time to tell him that someone was waiting at the window of A3 with a dummy that should be treated as a casualty and carefully brought down. However, as he got to the top the ladder began shaking violently and 'our man' lost his nerve. As he hesitated, the chap with the dummy lost his grip and it came crashing down onto 'our man'. Only it was not a dummy. As a joke someone had swapped the dummy for a full-size skeleton from the lecture rooms. When it fell onto 'Our man', it scared the living daylights out of him. The skeleton fell to the ground, leaving 'Our man' frozen; then to add to his misery the extended ladder jammed and it took the best part of an hour to get him safely down to terra firma.

Mark Robberts

Strict but kind

I joined as a young Probationary Sick Berth Attendant in September 1964 and then qualified as a Medical Assistant in March 1965 with the transition of the Royal Navy Medical Branch. I left training division (TD) with many memories of early starts, cleaning stations and even working on Saturday mornings and marching back and forth from Canada Block to TD, situated where the Submarine Museum is now. I even served punishment one day for a misdemeanor and that meant extra duty of cleaning the steps to the Training Matron's Office.

I had the pleasure and even temptation of being in the last class to be both SBAs and Naval Nurses in training. One memory is that of being like brothers and sisters, which brought about many lasting friendships and indeed memories.

Being placed on the wards became an extension to training under the guidance of many nursing sisters of the Queen Alexandra's Royal Naval Nursing Service (QARNNS) and also the older male Medical Assistants and Medical Technical staff, many who had served in the Korean and Suez campaigns. The nursing sisters could be strict while at the same time being kind – my first ward sister even gave me a nurse's dictionary at Christmas and in turn taught me to care and even how to deal with the loss of a patient, my first experience of death.

On one early set of nights I sat holding hands with a young nurse, both of us somewhat scared of being on nights in a dimly lit and creepy hospital. The nurse in question was eventually to become the Matron in Chief of QARNNS.

The old 'A' block was not fully refurbished until 1970 and until then on night duty one had to walk through an old ward with one single light bulb swinging back and forth in the breeze from a broken window: the place was full of shadows and stories abounded. I would walk quickly and not look back, whatever the creepy noise.

One sister while on night duty would ride a pusser's 'red devil' – the name for the red bicycles that were all over the dockyard and naval establishments – between the main hospital and Zymotics, the ward for infectious diseases, carrying an old walking stick in case of attack. The sister in question, Blodwyn Gummer, is the only female ever to threaten to put me across her knee for various misdemeanors I had committed, but on night duty she would allow you a coffee break and take over from you if there was time.

Of course there was always the old game of locking junior nurses in the chapel of rest. At a staff re-union a few years ago an elderly grey-haired lady stormed up to me and poked me in the chest. "Eric Birbeck," she said, "I have never forgiven you for locking me in the Chapel of Rest at two in the morning." It had been at least 50 years ago, so we hugged and all was forgiven.

Some nights the metal bier was very noisy and the lid rattled, so one had to push and the other sit on top to ensure peace and quiet.

In the days of smoking, even on wards, handover reports to the oncoming staff by the sister meant getting use to Capstan Full Strength (if you smoked) with many a young lad thinking himself grown up but turning green after the first puff.

One comical event was a young Medical Assistant stepping out from between the pillars of the quadrangle to salute a senior surgeon who was riding a bike from the medical mess to the Arcade. The surgeon returned the salute and then wobbled the handlebars and shot onto the grass and upended into the rose bed.

Many a new young member of staff was fooled by being asked to go to another ward and ask for a 'long stand', and to be kept waiting for a while … as that was a long stand. Another was to go to stores and ask for a Fallopian Tube. The tube in question is part of female anatomy, so it was one way of learning.

Eric Birbeck

Everyone knew each other

I worked at Haslar as a nurse between 1998 and 2008. I was in Main Outpatients and loved it. I remember walking the corridors to the wards and to the Spar shop. In my younger days I even remember doing work experience on an orthopaedic ward in 1986.

Everyone knew each other and you couldn't walk down a corridor without saying hello and having a chat. The friendliness and happiness of the place will remain with me forever.

Caroline Churcher

Look – no hands!

Running from the old post office and D block was a wall in which there were two openings, a larger one for motor vehicles and a smaller one for pedestrians. A very tall Surgeon Commander rode around the hospital grounds on a 'sit up and beg' Rudge bicycle. His height obliged him to take the larger opening. One day approaching this opening at speed a Sick Berth Attendant saluted. The officer returned the salute, forgetting he had case notes under his other arm. Without a hand on the handlebars he was out of control. He tried to get through the smaller opening, too small for his height and finished unconscious in a heap with a shattered face and a scattering of case notes.

Mark Robberts

A remarkable memory

My late grandfather William Woodward DSM, after serving 35 years in the Royal Navy man and boy, worked at Haslar Hospital as an Officers' orderly between 1945 and 1964 when he retired. My father William Woodward Jnr – now aged 90 – recalled these three stories his father told him about his time there.

The first one was about a Lt Commander who broke his arm. On the morning of his discharge his car wouldn't start, so he tried the starting handle to get it going … which then kicked back at him and broke his arm again. Back into hospital he went!

The second was about Admiral Cunningham who, although betting was illegal in those days, asked my grandfather to put on bets for him.

The last memory was the time Lord Mountbatten visited Lord Cunningham and saw my grandfather and immediately said: "Bill Woodward, HMS Duncan, 1924", which proved what a remarkable memory Lord Mountbatten had.

Sally Cleal

Chance meeting on the ward

On 26 September 1966 my father Ken Baker joined the Royal Navy and after six weeks' initial training he went to RNH Haslar as a Probationary Medical Assistant. On 15 May 1967 my mother, Norma Baker (then Norma Brettell) arrived at Haslar having joined QARNNS.

That year, my father spent a weekend standing in for another Probationary Medical Assistant, Johnny Chetey, on E4 (medical ward) and this is where he and Norma first met. They subsequently did nights on different wards and as my mum walked back to Portsmouth train station my dad carried her case. They got on a train to London together. After two weeks' leave they met again in the NAAFI: my dad told my mum that he had bought a car and they agreed to meet at the Haslar Club. They started courting.

Dad was drafted to HMS *Ganges* in February 1968 and then came back in May to HMS *Daedalus* leaving my mum at Haslar. On 8 November 1969 they got married in Edmonton in London and after a joint draft to Malta in 1971-1972 my father was posted back to Haslar. My dad did his nurse training in Haslar during 1975-1978 and

Jackie's mother, Norma Baker, is pictured far left, in her early Haslar days

commissioned Medical Services Officer in November 1981, which was his first job back in Haslar. He then went onto become Deputy Redevelopment Officer in Haslar until July 1982 when he went to the Institute of Naval Medicine, but he went back to Haslar as Training Officer and then Principal Training Officer based in Haslar until 1991.

Both me and my brother John were christened in St Luke's and on 13 April 2002 in St Luke's I married Neil Bradbury.

Jackie Bradbury

A real career 'path'

My pre-QARNNS experience was predominantly in theatres. Naturally on entering QARNNS, in November 1970, I was given a Sister's post on a medical ward! After a few months I was given the post on the Female Surgical ward, a little closer to my speciality, but still with conscious patients!

One of these was Dame Matilda Goodrich, a formidable lady, especially to a wet-behind-the-ears Nursing Sister.

During my ward round one day, Dame Matilda said she'd really like to see the Rose Garden opposite the Sister's Mess. As I had the afternoon off I offered to wheel her across and during our visit she told me why she wanted to see it.

Dame Matilda Goodrich, matron of Haslar from 1944 to 1947 – a formidable woman

As a very junior Sister in Haslar she would cycle to Stokes Bay, load up the basket on her bicycle with flat stones and bring them back. Being interested in gardening she had noted there was no easy access to the rose garden, so she began laying the stones as a path. Each free afternoon she did this, a few stones at a time.

Miss Goodrich realised that all her colleagues were bring given appointments to various hospitals and establishments but not she. Daring to approach the Principal Matron, she was told it was not convenient to appoint her elsewhere at that time.

She kept cycling to Stokes Bay.

Plucking up the courage once again, she enquired about a posting and was sent away with a flea in her ear.

She kept cycling and more Sisters were given appointments.

Eventually she knocked on Matron's door and demanded to be told why she was being overlooked. Matron sent her to the Medical Officer in Charge. With her knees knocking, she asked why she was not being given an appointment.

His reply was, " My dear Miss Goodrich, how can you expect us to appoint you elsewhere until you finish the path?"

Of course she did finish it and duly received an appointment, one of many, and her career saw her awarded the DBE (making her a Dame), RRC (Royal Red Cross) and Bar (a repeat award for service).

I'm delighted to say that on our visit that afternoon she saw her path. Where is it now, I wonder?

Ellen Seward (née Kirtley)

Don't rip the baize!

My father was a doctor in the Royal Navy and we lived in The Terrace at Haslar on a couple of occasions. As kids we would have great fun in the grounds, I remember a huge air-raid shelter in between The Terrace and St Luke's. We used to go down into it: there were loads of wooden bunks inside, all covered in bird droppings.

The first house we lived in at Haslar was a flat – number 7 I think – in 1970 when we returned from Malta, then in about 1978 we moved to number 5, which seemed very grand and had an amazing cellar that we turned into a gang hut. The house had a big garden and an outside toilet. The tableware all had the Naval crest on it and the furniture was all married quarters stuff as we were between houses.

Between these times we lived in The Avenue and used to go to St Luke's every Sunday. We always went to the Officers' Mess for drinks afterwards and we loved ordering pineapple juice and putting it on my dad's chit then playing billiards, but always under pain of death if we ripped the baize. There were always loads of kids around Haslar, doctors' children mostly, and it was a fun place to live.

I went to Alverstoke Junior School when it was brand new, before prep school. During the holidays, if my brothers were away at school, dad would take me to work with him. He was a radiologist and the X-ray department was where I would spend my day. There was an endless supply of yellow paper that the X-ray film came out on and every colour of Sellotape, used for marking different patients X-rays … and dad had a swivel chair!

When my brother was about 18 he had a summer job gardening in the grounds, but mostly he told the lads from the borstal what to do and then lay in the sun. My other brother and I would search the grounds trying to catch him sleeping! I remember doing trampoline classes at Haslar. They were held outside and run by the PT guys. All of our babysitters were Wrens and my mum still is in touch with one, Veronica – in fact, I was her bridesmaid.

Caroline Blades (née Soutar)

Injustice still upsets me today

At my first Christmas in Haslar, which was 1981, I was the youngest nurse and probably the shortest too! I got to stir the Christmas cake mix and had a photo taken with matron and the youngest male rating and it was put in the newspaper.

One upsetting time in Haslar was when a rating was charged for a crime and we all were called together (practically the whole of Haslar ratings and officers) and it was announced what this person had done. Unfortunately she had the same surname as my maiden name and because she was popular and was well liked and I was new to Haslar and unknown, everyone thought it was me! Even though she was marched in front of us all, people just could not believe she had committed this crime. People even went up to my friends and asked how they could be friends with a 'thief'.

To this day, it still upsets me and I feel the injustice of it all. The same girl went far in the Navy because of her popularity.

I thoroughly enjoyed my time in Haslar, especially sliding down the curved banisters. I had a lot of fun and was very sorry to be disabled out.

Berny Webster

A rogue spark

My dear dad, Roy Loader, worked for the Ministry of Public Buildings and Works in offices based in Haslar, from the late 1950s to about 1979. It was a small yard right in the top corner to the right of the Main Gate. I remember going in with him on a Saturday morning and washing his car while he worked. We lived in Waterloo Road, just outside the far wall of Haslar and spent most of our summers swimming at Haslar wall beach. I can remember seeing the patients out on the balconies of the wards, brought out to get some air.

I have very fond memories of the annual Dockyard Christmas parties and the firework displays held in the hospital grounds. I remember one year, about 1965, when my younger sister was hit in the ankle by a rocket. A rogue spark had set off all the fireworks at once and people were sent running and screaming in all directions.

I worked at Haslar myself, as a cleaner in the 1980s, when my daughter was young. I worked every evening from 5pm to 8pm cleaning the recovery area outside the theatres.

Christine Allen (nee Loader)

Singing the 'golden oldies'

From 2002 to 2006 I worked for BNA, a nursing agency, as an auxiliary. I spent a lot of that time on the wards at Haslar and they were the happiest times of my entire 20 years in the care sector.

The four wards that I worked on most were A6, the breast cancer unit, orthopaedics, and the 'winter overflow' ward.

A6 was for patients suffering from stroke or head injuries; the staff were amazing and I felt privileged to work alongside them, I learned many techniques that I later shared at other hospitals – techniques that were unknown to their staff. I fully believed that if you were in that desperate situation that was the ward to be on with a great chance of walking out. As this was mostly for patients under 65 it was for me the most complex, as many were my age or younger: it brought home how vulnerable we all are and how quickly life can change.

The breast cancer unit was another amazing ward; the compassion and understanding shown was second to none. It was made into a close family type unit where the women supported each other and it had a kitchen/ lounge area set up to make them feel human and normal, unlike the clinical wards of most hospitals. I escorted some very frightened ladies to theatre, doing my best to keep their minds elsewhere for a short while hopefully they went on to a full recovery.

On the Orthopaedics ward, which was mostly for hip and knee replacements, time and patience were given throughout every stage.

The happiest six weeks I spent was on a ward that was opened to take the winter overflow of elderly patients from Queen Alexandra hospital in Portsmouth. It was manned entirely (except for me) by military staff, who told me they were used to active duties with soldiers not the elderly, so were happy to share my experience along with their expertise. They were the most happy, cheerful yet precise team I have ever had the pleasure to work with: everything was done with military timing.

One day I was humming to myself, as I often do, and one of the patients joined in. Before we knew it all the patients and staff were singing – we went right through all the golden oldies while still doing all the tasks required. Because the military staff were so efficient, we seemed to get everything done much quicker and this left time for the good things like leg massages. The patients all appreciated this simple but effective treat.

Radiance McLaren-Draper

Above: 1942 - QARNNS Nursing Sisters walk out in their new style outdoor uniform. Below: Training Division A Class 21 in September 1969, with Sister J Harvey

Above: a QARNNS Nursing Sister with VADs during World War II.
Right: Olga Franklin presents the Rose Bowl to Sister Janet Stephenson, winner of the 1959 Franklin Tennis Tournament

Birthday surprises

There are two things I remember while I was in theatres at Haslar, both involving Surgeon Commander Ian Jenkins and his birthday. The first was making him a cake in the shape of a patient on the operating table in the lithotomy position (a position of the legs in stirrups for surgery).

The second was finding out he liked sherbet fountains and spending the afternoon in the anaesthetic room making a giant sherbet fountain out of a three-foot cardboard tube.

Pete Williamson

Best foot forward

My father, Leonard Hillier, who passed away on 9 January 2017 spent many years working at Haslar as a Patrolman guiding traffic and personnel in and out of the Main Gate, while my mother Sylvia also had a career at the hospital working firstly in the Sisters' Mess before transferring to become a Theatre Orderly.

Over 6-7 May 1983 my mother and father, along with 26 other civilian and service personnel, set off from Haslar, putting their best foot forward to take part in a 67-mile sponsored walk through Hampshire. They were hoping to raise enough money to purchase and train a guide dog for the blind. The walk was begun by Surgeon Captain John Drinkwater RN, and many other staff gathered to give them a tremendous send-off.

Len and Sylvia can be seen at the front of the photograph, hats on and walking stick in hand, ready to set off

My parents completed the walk, taking in Romsey, Hursley, Winchester, Wickham and Fareham before returning to Gosport. They raised the grand sum of £52, which was indeed quite a tidy sum back in those days, all of which was donated to the charitable cause.

My father wrote an ODE TO THE THEATRE about the operating theatres at Haslar: he had a passion for writing and poetry and believed in his words that if you 'set your imagination free you can be anyone, or anything, or anywhere you want to be'. He always signed his 'From The Pen of Len'.

ODE TO THE THEATRE

Though my life is not in your hands,
Nor the decision to live comes from you,
I do not hesitate to say that I am pleased
that in reality you do exist.
For, without you, I am sure that a lot
of people would not be alive today.

But, though I praise you alone, I realise
that without the staff, the various machines,
and all the equipment in your bowels,
you would be a useless shell held up by beams,
but without you where would we be,
we, the lifesaving teams?

'From the Pen of Len'

Jane Brewer

D Day: we prayed for God's help

In the early months of 1944, a Blood Transfusion Unit was formed at Haslar. I was a VAD and a member of that Unit, and took blood from donors. At first, blood was taken only from Naval personnel, then, when it was realised that we would need a large blood bank, Navy vans toured Gosport and Portsmouth seeking blood donor volunteers from among the civilian population.

As the invasion date approached, the Unit trained in secret in the hospital cellars, learning about blood groups and blood transfusion techniques.

We were confined to the hospital for three weeks before D Day, and we were not allowed to send letters or make phone calls. We were issued with wide oilcloth armbands, which were white with a large red cross motif. The hospital transferred current patients to other hospitals inland.

There was a great sense of excitement and awe as the armada of invasion vessels assembled in the Solent. When off duty, we would wander over to the seawall to watch the spectacle. One day, when the King came to review the fleet, all the ships were dressed in flags.

After all the noise of embarkation, there was an eerie silence on the morning of 6 June when we awoke to find all the ships had sailed.

The first wounded arrived on 7 June. At first all was quiet and slow, then an enormous rush – no time to think or hesitate. Stretchers were being carried in by the Navy and the Army. Due to the degree of activity at the landing sites, this rush of patients had lain on the beaches until such time as they could be loaded on board ships to be brought to us. We had to cut the wounded out of their uniforms and dump the uniforms on the deck to be collected by the Sick Berth Attendants for incineration. We had to clean sand out of wounds and out of patient's hair. The sand lay so thick underfoot that it felt like walking on the seashore.

We worked 12-hour shifts, not watches, and of course did not go off duty if the wounded were still arriving on the ward. When we did go off duty we used to retire to St Luke's Church in the hospital grounds, where the organist would play us soothing music. We would say prayers for the men whom we had just left and ask God for his help on the morrow. None of us could face food immediately after coming off duty.

Mabel Halewood (née Packer)
Supplied by QARNNS Archive

A priceless reward

I was a volunteer guide at Royal Hospital Haslar for several years, showing people where to go for their appointments and helping staff if required. It was a pleasant, undemanding job where I met many people and often my own friends who came for a medical appointment in one department or another. There were twenty volunteers altogether, two for each weekday morning and afternoon, but we invariably teamed up with the same person. Wearing navy blue tabards we worked alongside the Friends of the Hospital and soon became their friends. My daughter worked in A&E for many years but had to transfer to the Queen Alexandra Hospital when Haslar closed.

I loved being recognised and waved through the gates having displayed my ID; the view of the beautiful well-kept grounds; the smell and sight of the sea and the feeling of great peace within the grounds – a priceless reward for our presence. A tour of the private houses where eminent medical and nursing staff lived was something outsiders would rarely enjoy. When we learned of the impending closure, we decided it could not possibly happen, not to this historic, valued and essential hospital. As the weeks went by it became clear that it would; ward furniture and equipment was spirited away and parking inside was plentiful. Staff disappeared and so did the patients; vacated rooms and wards soon gathered dust.

There was less to do and we were allowed to explore. I found the 'cabin' where I was cared for as a patient and another which had been used by my daughter. I also discovered the men's ward, which brought back memories of when my father died having been cared for by the wonderful nurses – a fitting place for a Naval man. On my last day I drove slowly past the gates (no friendly uniform to wave me through), along the beautiful road with rose bushes bordering well-kept roads. I dared my memory to fail me in the future. There was a last look at the sea-wall that had protected the hospital; then the bandstand; the building where members of Queen Alexandra's Royal Naval Nursing Service had lived; the Captain's residence; lovely St. Luke's church and the unforgettable burial ground; Haslar Terrace which senior staff had occupied, and the landmark and famous Water Tower – just a few of what Royal Haslar had offered over the years.

We, like so many others, attended the picnic-Proms, an event held in the grounds, which was in the nature of a farewell. Haslar cared for us all, more of the population than we shall ever know. I wish someone who mattered had cared for Her.

Evelyn Love

Brave men

I was in QARNNS from 1971 to 1987. When I was working as a nurse in Recovery in the Operating Theatre, during the Falklands War in the summer of 1982, I remember the wounded men coming off SS Uganda and being sent to us in Haslar. There were a lot of them, some very badly wounded, and most of the men were very young. There were many kinds of wounds, including burns and shrapnel. It was a very busy time and we all worked long hours. Most of the men were very badly wounded, but they were all so brave. I will never forget them.

Bridget Pelling

G'day girls!

In the spring and early summer of 1969 I was undergoing Part 2 Medical Assistant Training in Training Division in 'Dolphin 2' as it was also known.

We were accommodated in M1 and M2 Messes, old wards in the one-time infectious diseases Zymotics blocks.

We were marched every morning to the Medical Branch Staff Quarters, or more correctly Canada Block, for breakfast and on completion of that we marched to Dolphin 2 in our classes for instruction/training. There were always two and occasionally three classes of Medical Assistants in training as the course lasted 16 weeks and a new class started every eight weeks.

All would be well until we left what was then the Main Gate and crossed the road, left wheeling into Dolphin 2, which all or partly belonged to HMS *Dolphin* Submarine Base and Submarine School.

The accommodation block immediately on the left in Dolphin 2 was for Australian submariners. They obviously started work later than us as there were always some hanging out of the windows of their block to give we Poms a good Aussie 'greeting' whenever we marched in or out.

The Trainee Naval Nurses I believe got more 'advice' from the Aussies than we did as they crocodiled past, the Class shepherded and protected by a Senior VAD ((Voluntary Aid Detachment) Nurse and her assistant who were there to protect 'their girls' from sailors!

David Rawson

Very Attractive Damsel

At the outbreak of World War II, I was working in London for the Australian Government and became involved with the supply by convoy of essential Australian products to the UK. In my 'spare time' I was an Air Raid Warden. But ever since my days as a Girl Guide when I had filled one arm with first aid and nursing badges I had wanted to nurse, so any other spare hours were spent as a Red Cross volunteer in the local hospital. I never needed sleep in those days! Nursing seemed to be an endless round of bed-pans – thirty-two beds in a female ward filled with air-raid victims and the sick. Matron didn't think it seemly to put a young female onto a male ward so when, at last, I obtained my release from Australia House and was posted to Haslar, shortly before D Day, a ward full of young men was a bit of a challenge. But at least I was used to the wounds of air raid victims and these were not unlike the wounds sustained in battle.

I was a VAD and perhaps I should explain that title. One definition was 'Very Attractive Damsel'. Other less respectable explanations – popular with the Navy – took the 'V' to stand for 'Virgin', leading to all sorts of ribald interpretations. In fact the letters ' VAD' actually stand for Voluntary Aid Detachment. This organisation was formed in 1909 to provide addition of nurses in time of war and was staffed by volunteers from the Red Cross, St John's and St Andrew's. Some 5,000 of us served with the Navy in WWII, in hospitals at home and abroad and in hospital ships. Many of us spent at least part of our time in Haslar. VADs bought their own uniform that included a great coat, a walking-out suit, shirts and hat, two nursing dresses, seven aprons, cuffs, caps and all the rest. We were paid £10 a month from which a sizeable amount was deducted for messing (ie bed and board).

In many respects we were treated as officers and enjoyed the privilege of first-class travel on the railways. But we were not allowed in the wardroom unless we wore civilian clothes, which most of us did not have with us, being limited to one peg for all our gear. No-one seemed to know the origin of this strange rule but it did give the Queen Alexandra sisters a clear run and some VADs were inclined to suspect that it was they who lay behind the restrictions.

I eventually arrived at Portsmouth Harbour where no pinnace was available so I, with another new recruit, crossed by ferry, caught a bus to Haslar and lugged our cases to the VAD quarters in D Block. We were standing in the hall wondering what to do next when a stentorian voice boomed from above: "What are you doing down there? Come up immediately." I felt about five years old and nearly ran back to London; bombs seemed the lesser evil. This was our introduction to 'Madam' Miss Waistall: she was Commandant of the VADs and ruled with a rod of iron. Heaven help anyone found with a trace of lipstick, or arriving late in quarters, not having signed in. But behind the fierce exterior was a heart of gold and she never failed to look after our interest and our welfare.

When, after D Day, some of us were invited onto a submarine for a trip round the harbour, her advice was: "Be sure to wear knickers with elastic in the legs."

Good advice – I had never seen so many upturned faces at the bottom of a ladder. Her job could not have been easy; VADs were from all walks of life – professional artists, landed gentry, the middle classes and families that, nowadays might be described as 'deprived'. But class didn't seem to matter and, by and large, we got along famously.

A VAD recruiting poster from the Great War

One of our number recorded how, after settling a French soldier into bed, she unpacked his kit bag and spilled a packet onto the floor, remarking to a nearby Sick Berth Attendant: "Why does he need so many finger stalls?" The SBA quietly led her aside and explained the mysteries of contraception.

Back to my first day! Because the VAD quarters in Haslar were overcrowded we were sent to a requisitioned girls' boarding school called Ambleside – now a block of flats – in The Crescent. The Crescent was known locally as Admirals' Row but the accommodation we enjoyed would not have impressed any Admiral – not even Nelson. Thirty girls shared one bathroom containing a bath, a washbasin, a sink for washing clothes and an ironing board. At least there was a separate toilet. Of course, no one was allowed to lock the bathroom door and it was thus that I learned that one of our colleagues was averse to washing: when she did, the tidemark above her collar had to be seen to be believed, and her elegant legs were spattered with black spots where she had concealed holes in her stockings with ink. Not one of Madam's favourites – but she was great fun.

Our first job on arriving was to erect our iron bunk bed, a bit like assembling a piece of flat-pack furniture without instructions. When we eventually climbed in we tried hard to lie absolutely still in case any movement caused the bunk to collapse and that it did – as we were climbing out next morning.

Madam's rule did not extend to the wards where we were ruled by the Queen Alexandra sisters. We were all under intense pressure and it would be unreasonable to expect that all would be sweetness and light. Some QAs understandably became impatient with our mistakes and this was of some concern because their assessment was a key factor in our gaining promotion to Senior VAD and raising our pay to £12 a month – less Mess fees, of course. In my own experience problems were quickly smoothed over and soon forgotten And, as for the patients, I could record a string of romances between them and VADs.

What we did have to accept was a good deal of risqué observations. We just gave back as good as we got and had a laugh.

There were, of course, some very sad moments. My own enduring memory is of a very young 18-year-old Welsh soldier just after D Day. His body was so shattered that he had to be suspended in a specially constructed hammock. He knew he was dying but his only concern was that his widowed mother should have a pension. I assured him would try for him and I only hope she did. At least he died at peace.

The pressure on the hospital after D Day was enormous, with patients of every nationality – including German – plus all three of our own Services. We were extremely busy and not allowed to leave the hospital except by back roads to our quarters. But, when off duty, we climbed the wall on the seaward side – in those days the wall was as high as it is now in Dead Man's Mile, though not festooned with barbed wire. From there we could see the ships bringing back the wounded. When at last we were allowed to walk along Stokes Bay we were amazed to find the beach covered with grapefruit skins. Who on earth could have authorised the transport of such luxuries when we were so short of essentials? But I suppose we couldn't deny the Yanks, even if we hadn't seen a grapefruit since 1939.

With so much tiring work and so much sorrow it was essential that we could enjoy some degree of recreation, so the dances and shows in the Errol Hall were very popular. I particularly remember Bud Flanagan giving a show to express his appreciation of the way in which we had nursed his son. Portsmouth, and even Gosport, offered a wider range of entertainment but were accessible only with a late pass – 11pm. This sort of expedition usually involved walking in the blackout – something I would not do now, though I never experienced trouble then, nor did I hear of anyone else being molested. Otherwise, we could always stay at home and try our luck with the solitary sink and a load of smalls. Or take a bath before the hot water ran out!

I left the VAD and Haslar in 1946, taking with me a host of memories and experiences that I still treasure: the pallor of the VADs working in the underground operating theatres; moving patients down to the basements on red alert – though you didn't get any warning of Doodle Bugs which were prevalent around D Day. I remember, too, missing the pinnace and having to run over Pneumonia Bridge and through Gosport's narrow streets to the open-decked ferry, and then, on the other side, running from the pontoon to the Harbour Station to catch the London train. On a weekend pass every hour was precious, and I will not forget the Navy bikes issued to us – dreadfully heavy and lacking a freewheel facility. The only way you could rest your legs coming downhill was to lift your feet from the pedals altogether. The problem was to restore them to their rightful place without skinning your shins!

There were tragedies and tears. There were jokes and laughs. But, throughout it all, there was the wonderful sense of comradeship.

After the war our VAD Association published a book of individual memories entitled:'We Were There'.

I'm glad I was.

Sylvia Bell (née Feetey)
This account was originally presented at
Gosport Discovery Centre in 2007
by Sylvia Bell, who passed away
in October 2016 aged 96

Kicking my foot on purpose

I worked at Haslar as a Dental Surgery Assistant in oral surgery/orthodontics. One day I hobbled into work with what I suspected was a broken foot. I limped around the surgery after phoning through to the staff's GP to get an appointment with Surgeon Captain Lambert, but unfortunately that was not until about 9.30am, so I hobbled around the surgery with my boss Captain Timothy Hall. He kept catching my foot with his foot while treating a patient in the dental chair – on purpose because he thought I had done nothing too it. I finally tottered over to the doctor's and he said: "Yep, I think it's broken. Take this note and go to X-ray."

I arrived there clutching my staff referral, only to be told I had to go to A&E (no privilege there either) so after sitting there for a few hours, getting seen and then getting referred to X-ray – which was opposite the oral surgery/orthodontist department – and then limping to fracture clinic, I finally returned back at work on crutches with my foot all strapped up because it was too swollen to plaster. My colleagues just said:

"You've been gone hours!"

I said: "I told you I had fractured my foot."

Three days later I was back at fracture clinic and had a plaster cast put on up to my knee and a shoe to wear. I went back to work, where my boss has me climbing up the stepladder to get patients' models down. Once again in surgery, he was still kicking my foot.

Typical, eh? As staff you just have too carry on!

I had fabulous times there, though. I worked there between 1993 and 1994 as a DSA, leaving as a Leading Wren, and then again from 1995 to 1996.

Jeannette Hunter (née Read)

Rent was 90p a day

In 2007 and 2008 I worked as a mammographer for the Patricia Massey Breast Screening Unit, sited in Eliza MacKenzie House at Haslar.

I was on a working holiday from Australia, and some of my fondest memories are of working at Haslar; the friendships I made have been long-lasting. I lived in the Senior Rates Mess, paying the princely sum of 90p a day rent – other staff lived in the Terraces, but the £1.50 a day rent to live there was too exorbitant for my backpacker budget.

In Eliza MacKenzie house, the mammography services took up the first floor, the clinical staff the second, and the administrative staff the top floor. The unit provided screening services for the NHS Breast Screening Programme, and diagnostic services for all women. The unit was one of the last to leave Haslar and relocated to QA.

As an Australian, I was often in awe of the hospital – I would often marvel that it was standing there as the First Fleet left for Australia all those years ago. Portsmouth holds some very fond memories for me – I met my husband there and returned to Australia with him.

Emma Woolley

Dancing on milk bottles

Prior to the Crosslink being built, the hospital matron had a small house near to what was then 'E' Block and the victualling office, facing into the Quadrangle. One evening the matron opened the front door and in fell a nurse and her Medical Assistant boyfriend who had used the doorway to kiss and cuddle. Many ex-staff will remember the cycle sheds being used as a trysting place late at night, also the patient airing grounds …

The Victualling office was where all food and drink deliveries were made and empty bottles stacked. One night the duty theatre staff (and I was one of them) was called to Sick Officers' Block. They ran from their night cabin on the top floor of 'B' Block, through F6 ward, down the two flights of stairs and out of the door by the Victualling office into pitch black night.

There was a sudden commotion and glass bottles bouncing everywhere; Petty Officer Medical Assistant Ted Littlewood was dancing on milk bottles underfoot and like an acrobat keeping his balance and getting nowhere and one could not run and laugh at the same time.

As Theatre staff we tried to keep ahead of the times; with the new service for cardiac arrest we were expected to attend all over the hospital. Having an increase in equipment, Chief Ken Scofield got hold of an old Silver Cross pram which was duly

The Breast Screening staff pictured in 2007: Linda Wale, Dawn Strudwick, Maz, Kate Hedger, Tina, Sarah Eke, Emma Grant, Lynn Lane, Che Piedt, Heidi Haskell, Sheena Nepaul, Claudia Makgatho, Liz

loaded with items of support and ready for the off. On a call it was taken to a lift for the appropriate floor and even over to Sick Officers' Block. There was a major drawback in that the prams was so well sprung that items would fly out and have to be recovered. After a few bad runs the pram idea was given up.

A well-known plastic surgeon used to hold surgery on a Saturday morning. One day the sister taking the operation turned to Chief Eddie Harrison.

"Chief – sterile ice please!" he said. It was to pack over the patient's nose.

Eddie went into the instrument room, placed a bowl of ice in the steam autoclave and then wheeled a bowl of steaming hot water into the theatre.

"Chief, I asked for sterile ice."

Eddie smiled: "Well, it was ice before it was sterilised."

During one evening duty we heard laughter coming from the X-ray darkroom next door to the theatres. A newly arrived patient complaining of stomach pains was X-rayed and in those days glass X-ray plates had to be processed in a dark room. The technician came out still laughing and showed us the plate. In the centre of the abdomen, surrounded by pelvic bones, was a small sailing ship and the shape of an Old Spice bottle on its side. Some people do poke things in strange places.

One procedure common at the time was for Surgeon Captain Bruce Victor Jones – Orthopaedic Consultant – and Surgeon Commander John Haughton, Consultant Anaesthetist, to undertake spinal manipulations under anaesthetic. The unusual aspect of this procedure was that it was carried out on a mattress placed onto the floor. No ordinary mattress, but a good old-fashioned horsehair 'pusser's navy single mattress' specially kept in a cupboard for such a procedure. The patient would be wheeled in, anaesthetised and the mask held in place by the anaesthetist. The patient, who would be lying on a canvas stretcher, was lifted off the trolley and lowered onto the mattress. Bruce Victor Jones, or BVJ as he was affectionately known, would then kneel beside the patient and would commence manipulation, twisting shoulders and legs, even turning the patient.

On one occasion the patient was much larger than BVJ (who was a slight man and short in stature) and in one manoeuvre the unconscious patient rotated and collapsed on top of BVJ, pinning him to the mattress, where upon John Haughton lay down beside BVJ and started to bang the floor shouting: "A-one, a-two!' as if he were a wrestling referee. BVJ then peered out from under the patient's armpit saying "That's not funny, John," while the rest of the staff collapsed in fits of laughter.

One establishment used by many male staff was the No Place Tavern in Stoke Road, run by Ben Bryant, ex-naval master-at-arms. Many on-call, duty staff would gather and should the phone ring then Ben would cry "Whose Duty?"

Another favourite was getting egg banjos (fried egg sandwiches) from the Cartoon Café in Bemisters Lane known as Squeeze Gut Alley and now the Royal Bengal. A volunteer would take a small case and get egg orders for hungry mates in Canada Block.

Many staff on night duty of two weeks on duty and then a week's leave would head to The Ark Royal or the George and Dragon for a few beers and then head back for bed before duty again.

The original Haslar Club was situated in the basement of Canada Block and was run by the NAAFI. It was the social nerve centre of Haslar for all junior staff. The highlight of the month was a dance, with new nurses being allowed to visit the club for the first time after not being able to visit in their first month. Sunday evenings were very busy with those coming back off weekend leave to meet friends.

Interport dances and events took place twice a year between RNH Haslar and RNH Stonehouse, Plymouth, following sporting events between teams from both hospitals. The dances were also held at the Errol Hall, also the scene of many dances for staff with pop groups of the time including The Bay City Rollers, Joe Brown and The Bruvvers and many more.

In the 1940 and 50s the BBC Light Programme would broadcast from Errol Hall with many stars of the day including Arthur Askey, Cyril Fletcher and Bud Flanagan, along with bands and orchestras to entertain staff and patients. One top American act of the day was the Memphis Boys who appeared on more than one occasion.

In the late 1960s a Folk Club was started in the cellars of C Block and became known as the C Minus One Club. In the short time that it was in use, Jasper Carrot made one of his first appearances.

With the new build of 1976, the Haslar Club moved from Canada Block to the west wing of the new build, which although it was larger and able to hold dances and events never seemed to have the air of the old Haslar Club.

Eric Birbeck

Eyes!

I was working as a young Medical Assistant in the Civilian Discharge Office, which also served as an information desk. One day the face of a rather brusque gentleman appeared at the hatch simply saying "Eyes".

There was also at that time an old and bold Chief Petty Officer Medical Assistant in charge of the office, who responded to the gentleman.

"Eyes, sir?"

"Yes, eyes," he responded, clearly failing to grasp that the Chief did not understand him. "Eyes," he said again. "Where is the Eye department?"

Clarity was established and the Chief gave him the somewhat complicated directions to the Eye department.

Some ten minutes later the gentleman appeared again saying:

"I appear to have lost my bearings."

"Ah bearings sir!" replied the Chief. "That will be the works office. You need to go to Zymotics, out the door to the far end of ..."

Bill Durning

A place for the perfect murder?

On being commissioned in 1982 I went back to Haslar as a young Sub Lieutenant and became the Assistant Redevelopment Officer. This meant I liaised between the hospital and the contractors who were building Crosslink – a new building in the centre of the hospital to house a new outpatient department, Accident and Emergency, an operating theatre complex and a dental surgery.

I was also given a few other hats, namely Sports Officer, Fire Officer and Small Business Contracts Officer. Life was never dull or boring as I always had something to occupy my attention.

Periodically I was called upon to carry out the duty as Officer of Watch, which was being responsible for all non-direct medical administration and management of the hospital during evenings and weekends. One Saturday afternoon I was sitting in the main hospital reception when an ashen-faced digging contractor came in and said that while digging a trench for the sewage pipes from Crosslink he had dug up a human skeleton. I went immediately with the man to an area at the back of the hospital called the paddock. I found not one but two skeletons, each of which were only about three feet down in the trench. I contacted the duty coroner and he asked me if I was aware of where the skeletons might have come from and if the area might have been an old cemetery. I suggested we call in Eric Parsons, the Hospital Librarian and Museum Curator, who I was sure would be more knowledgeable about the Paddock.

From documents in the Hospital Library we learned that the Paddock had been used many years ago as a burial ground not only for deceased sailors from the hospital and hospital ships moored in the harbour but also from Sir John Moore's army, who had camped there having returned from the Battle of Corunna. Most had died from typhus and yellow fever. Mr Parsons estimated that there were thousands buried in the Paddock. The duty coroner left with a smile saying "don't call us, we'll call you." I remember for a long time afterwards I told people that if they wanted to do away with the mother-in-law then to do it now and bury them in the Paddock – no-one would ever find out.

In 1987 I was again Officer of the Watch when I was awakened to be told that there was a bit of a gale blowing which was damaging the hospital building. I got dressed and began to walk – or rather, fly – around the grounds in what turned out to be a hurricane. Two very old trees had been uprooted. Some windows had blown in, causing extensive internal damage to the medical typing pool. I watched slates being blown off the roof and hurtling around the grounds. I immediately instructed reception and the main gate staff to stop anyone walking or driving around the grounds and to forewarn the ambulance station of the danger when bringing patients to the hospital. The following morning brought calm back to the hospital, though there was a lot of clearing up that had to be done.

Michael Raven

Two late-night passes a week

I trained at Haslar from 1962, and then returned in 1965 from Malta to complete my training and spend a year as a staff nurse.

I always remember that when we returned from Portsmouth after a night out, we would stop at the bus cafe – more like wooden hut – for a fried egg roll costing sixpence (two-and-a-half pence in today's money) to eat on the way back over Pneumonia Bridge. Believe me, in mid winter it was very cold. I remember Miss Beasley who looked after the student nurses. We had two late-night passes until 11pm per week, which increased to midnight after we had passed our preliminary exams. She would come round every night and shine her torch on every face in the cabin to make sure we were adhering to the rules.

At Christmas we would turn our cloaks inside out – they were lined in red – and visit the wards to sing carols.

We had to walk through HMS *Dolphin* to our training rooms, with all the submariners wolf-whistling at us (we secretly liked it).

We were expected to be professional at all times and had to address any staff on the wards by their title and surname. I was caught one day by a very severe Sister, spraying my laddered stocking with Nobecutane that was used for sealing wounds. My last pair until payday. A terrible sin!

We started off with a basic blue overall dress looking more like lavatory cleaners, so when we were given our proper uniform we were delighted. Three dresses, fourteen aprons, three sets of starched cuffs collars and frillies, and three caps that became a work of art to fold. Even more difficult when you had to wear them in high winds because the back part used to act like a rudder.

We had to be inspected by the Matron of the Training Division and when it was my turn she made me bend over her desk to tell me my dress was too short and that she could see my stocking tops, so it was back to re-hemming that evening and I had to be rechecked the next day.

Rosemary Brooks

A family affair

While serving at Haslar, I was privileged to marry Yvonne Richards, a member of a Haslar family. Her mother Amy ran the staff NAAFI bar in the Haslar Club and the Senior Rates Bar in Canada Block, where I first met Yvonne. Bob, her father, was the Victualling Officer from the 1970s until 1993. Martin, her brother, was a driver of ambulances and staff cars and at the time of writing this, he is now a member of the Security Team.

Not to be forgotten was Yvonne's grandmother, Susan Richards, who was a cook in the Sick Officers Quarters between the two World Wars. There are many Gosport families who can make this claim of the entire family working at Haslar.

Like many staff and Haslar families, we were married in St Luke's church in 1972. Sadly, also like so many, Yvonne's memorial service was held there too and her ashes lie in the Memorial Gardens, only yards from what was her family home in Clayhall Road.

Eric Birbeck

A learning curve

Let me set the scene … the severe winter of 1962/1963, where in D block dormitory there was ice on the inside of the windows. Shivering PNNAs gathered around the one convector heater. Yes, this was Jenner Class, joining the Royal Navy to administer compassion to all the lovely sailors! We trotted over to Dolphin Torbay block every morning and for six months were instructed by Royal Naval Sisters, Chiefs, Petty Officers and Hookies (Leading Hands), plus one Scottish civvy gentleman who endeavoured to teach us names of useful drugs.

During this period we were let loose on real patients for one whole week. My friend Liz and I were dispatched to ENT (Ear Nose and Throat) Ward where, on reporting to Sister (God), were told to give a bed bath to a young chap who had had an eye op and to find the Chief (one step down from God) for help.

Knees knocking we approached Chief and asked for a trolley to set up all our requirements, as instructed in classroom by Sister Tutor. After being told that we were in the real world now, we were pointed in the direction of a curtained area with a flannel and plastic basin. We did our best and the very cheeky young patient assisted with certain parts of his anatomy.

Day Two and we were back again on ENT Ward, feeling like old hands now, only to get sent to the Operating Theatre. What excitement! Off we trotted and found a door with 'Operating Theatre' on it. We were given masks, wellies and gowns and were all ready for … hang on, I thought, that's a funny place to keep your tonsils. Yep, you've guessed it – wrong theatre! Oh well, at least we learnt how to strip out varicose veins. Too scared to do or say anything we stuck it out for the morning. Next day when the ENT surgeon did his rounds he commented on not seeing Liz and I in his theatre the previous day, so we just said he probably hadn't recognised us due to our masks.

The rest of the week passed and we returned to lessons, then after our sixth month we all got drafted to RNH Stonehouse and then to Bighi in Malta where I finally saw tonsillectomies performed and guess what? They are not in your legs!

Maggie Feist

Hunt the file – a team effort!

I worked at Haslar for 17 years. As an Administration Assistant, my first position was in the MMP office (Medical Provisions Point). I was responsible for supplying all medicines and drugs ordered by all HM Ships, Bases, including abroad, and the hospital. It was a very busy and demanding job as orders came in constantly by request forms and telephone calls. The work consisted of a card system and all entries were handwritten. After two years the office was moved out of the hospital and taken over by an establishment in Aldershot and one admin assistant was surplus to requirements. I volunteered to transfer as I wanted to continue to work within the hospital.

My next job was in the Pharmacy Department as an assistant to the head pharmacist. I worked there for six months and then transferred to the Ophthalmic Department where I was promoted to Administration Officer. My work in that department consisted of reception desk duties, running daily clinics and making follow-up appointments, dealing with telephone calls, and collecting and preparing patients files ready for their appointment.

I was also responsible for dealing with all referrals received from General Practitioners, opticians and forces Medical Officers and passing them on to the consultants and specialists. They would be returned to me for me to make the patients' appointments. Cataract surgery was performed on patients in the hospital theatres until the hospital was taken over by the NHS. All surgery was then transferred to the Queen Alexandra Hospital.

All the civilian staff working in the hospital worked as a team when it came to finding a mislaid patient file. We would go from one department to another chasing up a file, as many patients attended more than one clinic. The working atmosphere within the hospital was great, and I enjoyed every minute that I worked there.

When my mother was 84, she broke her hip and was admitted to the hospital for surgery and treatment. Due to the excellent caring staff she made a full recovery. Two years later, she was admitted for a gallbladder operation and again made a full recovery.

My grandfather, Oswald Charles Samuel Stares (ex Royal Marine based at St. Vincent barracks), worked as a gardener in the grounds of Haslar after serving in the first world war. He retired in 1939 and was presented with a clock for his services. My brother Kenneth still has the clock and the inscription reads:

'Presented to O. Stares from the Officers and Men of S.C.E's Dept Haslar, on his retirement after 20 years service. Dated 14/04/39.'

One lasting memory to share is the 14 years my husband spent under the care of various departments within the hospital, after his first heart attack at the age of 42. His health started to deteriorate from this point, and as his visits became a regular occurrence they became to be known as 'holidays'. Through the time spent with the staff and consultants at the hospital, our family ended up on first-name terms with staff, and the treatment he received was of the highest standard: my daughter Karen and I owe our deepest thanks to them. All this was taking place while I continued to work at the hospital.

Sylvia Wrightson

War postponed our wedding

I arrived at Haslar in January 1981 to work as (what was then) a Senior Nursing Sister in QARNNS. I had trained and worked as a civilian nurse in various roles for the previous ten years, so this was going to be quite a bit different. That first night there was a Twelfth Night party in the Sisters' mess, so I was definitely 'in at the deep end'.

My room was on the top floor of the mess overlooking the site of the wreck of the Mary Rose so I was able to keep a distant eye on proceedings out at sea.

My most enduring memories of Haslar are centered on the Falklands War. I had met my husband-to-be, dental surgeon Steven Reeves, in May 1981 and we were engaged several months later. Steve joined HMS *Glamorgan* in October and in April 1982 she was one of the first ships to be sent straight down south from Gibraltar when the conflict started. I vividly remember the ghostly atmosphere around the wards at Haslar and the hushed murmurings as preparations were made for staff to join a hospital ship. On the morning of 5 April 1982 I stood in uniform on the sea wall to watch the task force sail into 'the unknown'.

HMS *Glamorgan* eventually limped home after being hit by a land-based Exocet with the loss of 14 men. I had had the job of rearranging our wedding, which had originally been planned for 22 May at St Luke's church at Haslar. Steve and I married two weeks after his return. We have one son, Simon, who was christened in St Luke's, so I have very happy memories of that little church despite the fact that Steve and I divorced in 1996. Sadly Steve died in May 2017 aged 61.

I also spent several days in Haslar as a patient myself so I have seen it from many different angles and now I often walk along the seafront, past the sad shell of what was once a wonderful hospital, with bitter-sweet memories.

Penny Reeves

Left: Medical Assistant Eric Birbeck as an operating theatre trainee in 1967. Right: Nurse trainees (left to right) Jo Escott, Margaret Meakin and Mary 'Josie' Davies about to go on Christmas leave in 1967

Give me shelter

During my first spell as Night Sister on B Block at Haslar in 1963 at around midnight on a very wet night, a Petty Officer from the Receiving Room (Casualty Department) asked me to see a lady who had arrived wanting overnight accommodation. The lady was very well spoken but bizarrely dressed. She claimed to be en route to a Territorial Army Camp in the West Country, said that her lift from Fareham had failed to materialise and, therefore, the Royal Navy was obliged to give her shelter. I thought if I could persuade her that she had a headache, I could send for the Medical Officer … but I did not feel entitled to extend Their Lordships 'hospitality'; nor did I fancy the idea of questions in the House of Commons as to why this 'Army lady' had been put out to walk to Gosport in the rain in the early hours of the morning.

Then I remembered the Matron's preface in the Admiral's Report Book, in which she invited us to call her at any time. On waking, Miss Burman asked if the lady was a Dr Barbara Moore, who had recently walked from John O'Groats to Lands End with some publicity.

It subsequently transpired that the lady was a prostitute, who had been turfed out of HMS *Dolphin* after a party. She insisted she was not asking for charity and showed us proof thereof – her handbag contained hundreds of pounds in notes.

Although, at Miss Burman's suggestion, we did find a bed – all efforts at finding local B&B establishments having been in vain – the lady decided she did not want to stay and went off with a passing policeman … which is how we found out what her real business was.

Mrs Panoecia Gaunt (nee Foster)
Supplied By QARNNS Archive

A 'scratch' private army

Following an assault / murder of a soldier in Germany by the IRA, Mrs Thatcher immediately directed the MOD that every military establishment would be guarded by armed personnel.

I was First Lieutenant with duties as Security Officer and also Duty Admin Officer at Haslar when during the next evening I was told to deploy armed sentries with immediate effect. This was a Friday. These things always happen on a Friday! Having conferred with Frank Golden, then Medical Officer in Charge, I sent a signal to the MOD to the effect: 'Thanks for the offer but we are a hospital. I have no trained personnel for guard duties, I have no weapons and certainly no ammunition so sorry, we can't play.' I presumed that would be the end of it.

On Monday morning a number of things happened. The MOD said we had no excuse. The Medical Director General (Navy) sent a signal directing that no personnel wearing red crosses (Medical Branch badges) were to be deployed, otherwise to go ahead and sort it.

I was asked what weapons I needed and by early afternoon I had two cases of new Sub Machine Guns and 10,000 rounds of 9mm ammunition. For three days this cache of arms lived in my office on the main corridor thereby increasing the security threat until I reached an understanding with HMS *Dolphin*.

I had also requested two 9mm pistols but I then had to go to HMS *Sultan* speak to a contact and came away with a pistol under the passenger seat of my car. I procured a webbing belt and holster from somewhere. Through HMS *Dolphin* I arranged weapon training for all non-medic ratings, both male and female, and by Wednesday I had a scratch private army suitably kitted out with camouflage-combats and webbing. I knocked out some standing orders for armed sentries; paraphrased they said 'don't touch the trigger or point the weapon at anyone unless there was a direct threat to staff or patients'.

Much to chagrin of the Supply Officer I was able to partially meet the directive and deployed two armed sentries, mostly from Supply and Secretarial – in other words, writers, cooks and stewards – around the clock for approximately six weeks. To fully meet MOD orders we also had to mount irregular armed security patrols. This was achieved by me and the Master at Arms patrolling in a clapped-out Land Rover. When on duty I carried my sidearm, so technically I was an armed medic.

After a while HMS *Nelson* sent over ratings for guard duty but I discovered they were P7R ratings (patients on light duty) Some of whom were having psychiatric treatment at Haslar and I had them removed and covered their duties with my team.

Things moved fairly quickly and the Commander in Chief of Naval Home Command organised a permanent guard force and subsequently armed MOD Police were assigned the permanent role.

One morning during this latter period the Duty Chief Petty Officer Medical Assistant bought a gun into my office and explained that there had been an accidental discharge without injury to anyone. On investigation it was discovered that, contrary to written orders, a young rating had decided to clean his weapon in the guardroom. Apparently he said: "I had a rush of shit to my brain and cocked and fired the rifle, placing a round between my mate's feet, sir."

He removed a six-inch disc of concrete from of the floor. Both men were lucky. The previous week a MOD policeman was killed in a similar incident. My miscreant was charged and went before the 'Captain's Table', a disciplinary hearing at Nelson. The penalty was not particularly harsh. It seems accidental discharges were quite common at the time.

The Commander in Chief's staff subsequently carried out an investigation and found Haslar's operational orders to be in order, and I was complimented on the efforts of my team, but the accident sped up the placement of armed MOD policemen on the gate. Once this happened the Medical Officer in Charge wrote to all at Haslar who were involved thanking them. I received a letter of commendation which I still have somewhere.

Tony Harrington

A severed head

When I was Supply Officer of Haslar Hospital during the 1980s I used to have to do rounds of the non-medical areas of the hospital, which included the large underground areas. At one time these had housed an underground hospital and in one of the spooky areas was a store with a lot of specimens in glass jars in formalin to preserve them.

There were some pretty nasty-looking tumours – incredibly large specimens because in those days people would not go to the doctor's and things just grew! There were three Chinese men's severed heads from the Boxer Rebellion, a violent anti-foreign uprising that took place in China between 1899 and 1901. There were a lot of beheadings during this conflict; I am not sure why these three heads were brought back to the UK, but there they sat all those years and I certainly did not fancy hanging around those glass jars just in case!

Glenn Duggan

Yes, Matron

I joined Haslar in 1976 having completed my initial training at HMS *Raleigh*. I was already a qualified nurse at the time but I still had to do my part two Medical Branch training. This was done in a building across the road from the hospital (now part of the submarine museum). I remember having to march over to the hospital to visit various departments and what struck me was the size of the building and – once inside – the immaculate cleanliness of the place. I was later to find out why when working on the wards, as the captain did 'rounds' when the place had to be spotless.

While going through my initial training, there were lots of different things for me to learn even though I was a qualified nurse, but one thing that stood out was the camaraderie amongst fellow serving medics. This was going to stand me in good stead for the rest of my 28 years' service.

One of the duties of the part two trainees was to provide fire crews within the hospital. If there was a fire someone would ring the bell, which was situated adjacent to St Luke's church and the fire party would collect a truck and – complete with firefighting equipment – run to the scene of the fire, pushing or pulling the truck. Luckily there were not too many fires and the local fire brigade was on scene within minutes of the alarm being raised.

My first days on the wards were filled with trepidation, as this was my first time in charge of a ward. However there were always more experienced staff at hand in the shape of the QARNNS sisters, some of whom you would not argue with! To this day I still wonder how they shaped their wonderful crisp white hats. Fridays were a day to remember as this was the day matron (those were the days when they ruled the hospital and woe betide anyone who crossed them) used to do her ward rounds. I remember walking round with them many times and you had to know quite a lot about each patient and no questions were expected to have a negative answer.

I worked on many wards during my time at Haslar, including time on the psychiatric unit where I was completing an assessment period prior to being considered for Mental

Health nurse training. I can remember after mealtimes on the unit having to collect all the waste food and taking it to a bin outside. The bin was collected daily and the swill was taken to feed the pigs on the adjacent farm, which was actually inside the hospital grounds. Unfortunately that did not last due to food safety regulations that were introduced.

One cannot be in the services without having to be duty officer at some stage, whether as duty senior or officer of the watch. This was a sleep-in duty where you were allocated a cabin on the ground floor of the mess. Many things could occur while on duty, from going to scenes of fires (usually false alarms thankfully) or checking out suspicious parcels. One of the episodes I will not forget was when two young nurses tried to get in through my window while I was asleep. Not the usual thing to happen, as more often than not it was ratings scaling walls and drainpipes to gain access to the female nurse quarters! On this particular night I was just dropping off to sleep when I heard a voice from outside the window calling 'let me in, let me in'. It was quite clear these two were worse for wear and were in the wrong place, as they were both junior ratings. Things were becoming a little silly when one of them tried to open the window. I decided to escort them from the vicinity for their own good. I promptly took them to the main gate and informed them that they needed to sober up and if they tried to get into the hospital again I would have no option but to report them to my superiors. Thankfully they did not return.

Haslar was not only recognised as a centre of medical excellence locally, nationally and internationally but also for the local social life. This ranged from the Medical Officers' annual cocktail party to the numerous mess dinners. The navy can always find something or someone to celebrate!

Fire crew and escape ladder at the ready at the old Main Gate

However, what sticks in my memory as junior rate is the renowned junior rates Haslar disco (affectionately known as the bop or cattle market). The queues for this outside the main gate on a Thursday were the talk of the town. The discos were held in the cellar or the Medical Branch staff quarters and were very well attended. This was more evident whenever a new class of nurses joined. Many relationships were formed or broken here and no doubt there are some (Haslar babies) still alive today.

Nigel Hockenhull

Clean floors ... and trimmer waists

Anyone in the navy will tell you that if you were asked to do something you did it – no questions asked. For nurses in the mid to late 60s in Haslar this included domestic cleaning (believe me, the place was spotless, inspected regularly by white-gloved Captains and Admirals). Many hours were spent 'bumping' the shining wooden floors – this involved swinging an extremely heavy weight wrapped in a blanket-like cover on the end of a long wooden pole from side to side over the whole ward floor till it positively gleamed. The extra bonus was that nurses ended up with much trimmer waists as a result.

Ultimately, outside cleaners were brought into some wards and we saw the end of the bumpers and the introduction of electric polishers. This, however, coincided with a national era of strikes (a totally alien concept to anyone in the Navy) and worker unrest in the civilian world. Our limited knowledge from newspapers, TV and gossip led us to believe that it was seriously dangerous to do a task that belonged to a civilian, so for some time there was a general fear of doing things that might upset the cleaners in case they all went out on strike. In typical naval fashion we would joke about it if we were so much as caught washing up a cup but, to be honest, to this day I have no idea if the cleaners even belonged to a union.

Happily, the civilians of Gosport were an amazing workforce, many having naval family connections themselves. They soon became a vital part of the ward teams and clearly loved Haslar as much as we did. In fact they, and the people of Gosport, fought for Haslar to the very end.

Edith Kinghorn

Best years of my life

The 13 years I spent working at Haslar were unforgettable and the best years of my life. I worked for five years in the Galley, and then in the grounds. I met some wonderful people – staff and patients – and I never wanted to leave. I owe it to Haslar for saving my mum's life – if it wasn't for them, she wouldn't be here today. I wish to God that I could go back. Happy times and of course bad times too, but overall I will never forget Haslar.

Andrew Newton

Sleeping in the igloo

My Service Number was W621313. I was called up on 18 February 1944 at the age of 19 as a Royal Naval VAD (Red Cross) at Haslar and I worked in the Medical Duty Cabin as a VAD Clerk. I wanted to sign up as a nurse but I was advised not to after an operation on my stomach.

I lived at Ambleside, St Marks Road, Alverstoke, where five of us shared one bedroom. Miss Irene Waistel was the Commandant in charge of VADS.

I worked for Surgeon Captain (later became Rear Admiral) Ingleby-McKenzie and every morning I typed up notes of the sailors who had been to see the doctor.

I spent Christmas 1944/45 there and can remember that there was plenty of Christmas dinner and food. Concerts were given and there were dances in Errol Hall.

A couple of month's later no-one was allowed within 10 miles of the coast and barbed wire was put down. All leave was stopped. Once D Day started all leave was cancelled and no-one was allowed any leave. However, one VAD was given a list of items that everybody needed and allowed out to do the shopping.

There so many boats in the harbour and in the Solent that it was often said you could walk all around Portsmouth and Stokes Bay and to the Isle of Wight without getting your feet wet! When D Day was about to happen, another VAD and I were picked to go on night duty at the hospital – same work but you stayed for 24 hours. We were given the cold room to sleep in, known as the igloo. This was so quiet we could sleep during the day.

VADs at Haslar in May 1946, with their Commandant Irene Waistell (centre), who served at Haslar during World War II and was known to the VADs as 'madam'

I can remember planes flew quite low over the Channel. D Day was put back a day due to the weather. If it had not happened on 6 June we would have had to wait another month due to the moon. When I woke up that morning and drew back the curtains there were no ships in sight; they had all gone in the night, So we knew D Day had started even before we got downstairs.

Casualties came to Haslar from the Normandy beaches. One of the first was a Daily Telegraph news reporter. The casualties stayed at the hospital or were put in ambulances or hospital trains and taken up-country.

I then became a Senior VAD and then a Supervising VAD 2 on each watch. I was on the port watch. I was part of the crew/staff in charge of VADS in Medical Duty Cabin.

Before things were returned to normal and leave was restored, only special leave was given and I had to submit a form to attend my brother's wedding. It was granted!

We were allowed to go to morning service at 11 o'clock on Sunday at St Luke's in the hospital grounds. Midnight services were in Holy Trinity Church.

I can remember there were two buses. One went past the cemetery and the conductor called out 'Haslar Underground'!

Peace was declared in May 1945 and I was demobbed in October 1946.

Evelyn Mary Heffernan (née Seward)

Everything is above the belt

For me it is history repeating itself. In 1944, my mother befriended the Wrens who came to our small village of Kingsdown in Kent. Some were very homesick and she helped them and gave them comfort in our home. One of them was getting married and asked me to be a Wren mascot for her wedding day; I was the only civilian there as it was an all military event, a great honour for a nine-year-old.

After the war, I was nursing for a few years in Kent before joining the British Red Cross and becoming a VAD, working in London, Surrey, Kent and Hampshire hospitals. It was while I was working at Knowle Psychiatric Hospital that I got a call asking me if I would like to do duties at the Royal Naval Hospital Haslar, I said 'yes' like a shot. It meant six buses a day to get there, but I was so glad to help the Navy. I was doing Beauty Care run by the British Red Cross, which is designed to help patients to relax and ease their pain. I did facials, hand and shoulder massage, make-up and manicures. I did this from 1980 till Haslar was decommissioned.

It was very strange working in a naval hospital; it was like being on a ship. The small wards were called 'Cabins', the restaurant was called the 'Mess', the kitchen was the 'Galley', the lavatories were the 'Heads' and so on.

One day I was walking down the corridor behind an old Admiral with two physiotherapists at his side and he was swaying a bit. One of physios would say "A bit to starboard, sir" and the other would say a bit later "A bit to port please sir." I must say this made me feel even more like I was on a ship.

In those days patients would stay much longer in hospital and the ladies wore pretty nightdresses. When I put make up on their face, if they wanted it, I would tone the eye shadow to match what they were wearing. One day a patient had put a towel around her shoulders before I could see what colour she was wearing.

"What lovely colour nightdress are you wearing today?" I asked.

She replied: "No eye shadow today, as I'm wearing a black nightdress and I think the doctors would think there's something wrong with me or someone has given me two black eyes."

We did have a good laugh.

I did another lady and when I had finished with her she was so delighted with how she looked that she jumped out of bed and started walking down the ward with only a flimsy nightdress on and pushing her drip stand. She called out to the other patients: "I look so great I'm off to a night club in Gosport". The other patients called out "Stop" before she managed to leave the ward. Everyone had a good laugh including her – it did us all good.

One time, I had a patient who was dying and she asked me if I could paint her toes bright red – we did not normally touch feet as part of therapeutic care. I asked the Sister if I could do them and she said yes. This made the lady very happy.

The Falklands was my first war at Haslar, but alas not the last. The hospital had a strange feeling during these periods because the wards were empty of civilian patients and the wards got ready to be filled by casualties from the war.

The first day I went into a ward of Falkland casualties, the patients in it asked me what a Red Cross lady did. I said "Massage" and they all cheered and looked delighted; they didn't give me time to say what else I did. I thought I must think quickly here, so I said: "Everything is above the belt" which was greeted with an "Oh" of disappointment. I went to one bed and a sailor started swearing at me. It went on for a bit and I think I was going slightly pink. Then he stopped and said "I do apologise, ma'am" and I replied "Don't worry, it has gone in one ear and out the other. Other patients say all sorts of things when they are in pain". Then he said "But why come to a bed with a name like that?" (my surname is FOST which stands for Flag Officer Sea Training in the Royal Navy) and "the sailors don't like what it stands for."

There was always banter between the Royal Marines and the Royal Navy. On another ward I did the nails of a very badly burned sailor whose nails had grown long and were digging into his palms, which can be very painful. This particular ward had a mixture of sailors and marines on it. I was treating this sailor and there were calls from a marine on the other side of the ward who called out about the sailors being 'soft' for being pampered. The poor sailor that I was treating said to me: "If only I could get out of this bed, I'd give him what for."

"Don't worry," I said, "I will get him back for you".

I went around the ward and eventually got to the bed that the marine was in. I sat down beside his bed and started talking about the Royal Marines, because I've had family in both the Navy and Marines and I know what they can be like together. I looked at his hands and they were very dry and the nails jagged, which is most uncomfortable when in bed. I took his hand and said:

"Would you like me to file your jagged nails?"

He agreed and after I had filed his nails I started to massage cream into his hands.

"Oh, this is lovely," he said. "Can you come back next week and do it again? My hands feel so much better".

My Navy chap chuckled and said: "Who's soft now?"

It was a good banter from one and all.

I was working on another day in the officers' wing and as in the rest of the hospital there were some bad cases. It was very hot weather and I suggested to my patient that he have a facial and massage saying to him "It will cool and relax you". At first he didn't like the idea but then said OK. I drew the curtains around the bed so it would be quiet and so he wouldn't be embarrassed, as I would be applying cream on his face and neck. I knew he was in a lot of pain and I hoped the treatment would help him. After twenty minutes, I could see that his hands, which had been curled tight on the bed beforehand, had started to relax. By the time I had finished he was in a deep restful sleep and the pained look on his face had gone. The Sister then came in and said to him:

"Do you want your pain relief medication, sir?"

He woke up and replied crossly: "What pain, I have no pain!"

This is when one feels good as a British Red Cross volunteer or an old VAD.

I have helped to give comfort to our brave men and women in all war situations over the 30 years I have worked at dear old Haslar, just as my mother did in Kent during the Second World War. I also sometimes helped in the welfare department and when my husband retired he worked in the hospital library.

Several years after Haslar closed, I was returning to a cruise ship after an excursion to St Petersburg when the gangway security guards, who were from Nepal, spotted me and stood to attention and saluted. They didn't do this for other passengers and when I asked them why they had treated me differently, they replied that they had never forgot the kindness and treatment that I had given one of their colleagues who was a patient at Haslar many years before. It gave me a big lump in my throat and I will never forget it.

Rosemary Fost

The saga of the pampas grass

My dear friend had a big vase of pampas grass in her room, as it was all the range then. She decided her vase needed one or two extra grasses. So we snuck out of D Block after midnight with coats over our night clothes to pick a couple from the back of St Luke's. Just as our mission of picking two was successful (from a patch where they would not be missed) we saw the Duty Officer in the distance. So we jumped in the middle of the pampas grass to hide. We never knew who that Duty Officer was but he seemed to be the slowest walker on record, and by then it had started to rain. I was beginning to think he knew we were there as he hesitated near St Luke's and I was imagining the trouble we would be in if he spotted us. Eventually he walked away and after a while, very wet, we ran back to D Block with our haul.

Hilary Butterworth

Were you ever in the Navy?

In late 1962 I was a naval physiotherapist at Haslar. One lunchtime two of us were covering the lunch break, when an old gentleman ambled in with a treatment card in his hand. The other physiotherapist took it, glanced at it and said:

"A B Cunningham. You're a bit old to be an AB (able seaman) aren't you, mate?"

"No" said the man, "actually they are my initials."

The penny still hadn't dropped, so my friend asked:

"Were you ever in the Navy?"

A cartoon drawn in the 1960s by 'Ning' Richards who worked in operating theatres and was a prolific cartoonist

The old man with a smile replied: "Yes, but a little bit higher than an AB. In my case AB stands for Andrew Browne, I'm Admiral of the Fleet, Viscount Cunningham of Hyndhope."

He had been in a car accident near his home, the Palace House in Bishops Waltham. I treated him for a month. He had a great sense of humour. I was walking him through the department one day and in one of the cubicles a young Naval Officer was demanding how he wanted his treatment.

Admiral Cunningham whispered: "Who's that?" I told him and with a smile on his face he pulled the curtains apart. "Who are you?" he asked.

"I'll have you know I am Lieut……!" said the officer. "And who are you?"

"Humph, I knew your father," said the Admiral. "He was just as noisy as you!" And walked on.

During his treatment he had been reading an historical novel and at the end of his treatment he gave it to me for my wife and autographed it for her. Sadly he died suddenly a few months later, but I still remember having the honour of treating him.

Tom Ladd

A Jacques Cousteau moment

Two memories stand out from my time at Haslar.

When I was a Probationary Medical Assistant in part 2 training, we were advised by our divisional chief to think about what we could study to gain an additional qualification to our Medical Assistant qualification. Someone then tricked a class colleague into putting in a request to do a muff diving course. The class leader did a great Jacques Cousteau impression of the "liddle muffs on the sea bed and how you had to treat them carefully, tempt them out with your tongue, etc." And Chief Webster shouted at us from the Training Department instructor's office window: "Who put you up to this?" How we laughed!

The same colleague answered the question "how do you diagnose pubic lice" with "on your hands and knees on the mess deck floor with a strong light and magnifying glass."

Another very important and lovely memory from my time there was of course, meeting my wonderful wife there and having both our children christened in St Luke's church.

Rob England

Teddy bear kidnap

I joined Haslar in the late 1980s. After completing my training I was posted to E3 Male Orthopaedic ward. It was a great ward as the boys were not so much ill as broken. We also had lots of civilian patients.

Forever Friends teddy bears were everywhere at the time. The matelots who were in-patients would be given them in bucket loads by simpering girlfriends. At night we would go round and nick them, leaving ransom notes such as 'two Mars bars from the NAAFI or the teddy gets it'. No matelot was prepared to chance not having his love token on show when the girlfriends came to visit. I blame this episode for any weight gain I had!

I remember E3 and my time at Haslar with such love.

Lena Hutton (née Scoular)

Wakey-wakey!

I remember in 1974, Training Division based in Dolphin II, the early morning runs, games of murder ball and many a freezing dip in the Solent off the Haslar sea wall – and all before breakfast. At least it ensured that no-one fell asleep during lessons!

Michael Wright

We had our own bank

I wonder how many people knew that Haslar Hospital had its own sub-branch of Barclays Bank? In the days when the banks were competing with each other for new accounts, Barclays Bank in Gosport High Street had three such sub-branches, one at Rowner Road, one at the helicopter repair base at Fleetlands, and a one-room operation at Haslar. The latter two operated for a couple of hours each, on a midweek day, Haslar over the late morning/lunchtime period with a cashier and a guard on duty. This was during the 1980s. The sub-branch operated from a room in a long corridor on the ground floor of A Block, close to what was then the Post Office and NAAFI shop, as you entered the Arcade having come through the (old) Main Gate entrance opposite the submarine museum.

I worked for Barclays at the High Street Gosport branch for two spells – one for a short time in 1975 and then as the office manager between 1981 and 1984. The latter period covered the Falklands Conflict, which in itself was a very interesting time with several of my cashiers having husbands in the Navy. As you can imagine, everyone was glued to the television and radio broadcasts as the conflict evolved and then their safe homecoming was a special time of celebration and joy.

On a more personal note, I have fond memories of Haslar for it was there, under the guidance of the Surgeon Commander in charge of the ENT department they diagnosed my Ménière's disease.

Bob Bottriell

An egg and a tin of soup

It must have been early in 1961 when I first encountered Haslar Hospital. I had enlisted in the QARNNS in 1960, aged 17. I planned to train as a nurse and was sent to the Royal Naval Hospital at Chatham but stayed there only for about three or four months as the hospital was scheduled for closure. My class (Cordington Class) of 16 hopeful trainee nurses was relocated in early 1961 to Haslar.We travelled by train to Portsmouth Harbour then by naval pinnace across the harbour to land at HMS *Dolphin*. From there we had a short walk to the hospital.

The nurses were housed in A block, a disused ward I imagine, and I shared a room with four other nurses. I don't recall if we were allowed to choose with whom we shared, but I do know that five of us were already firm friends. Later, as we became more senior, we all had our own rooms.

We used to go over to HMS *Dolphin* to join trainee sick berth attendants for more basic training.

I enjoyed most of my time at Haslar and worked on F2 Orthopaedic, E2 Female, C3 Medical, B2 Surgical, Officers' block twice – once on days and once on nights – and in theatres. Night duty was a bit harsh: we did 14 nights and then had two days to recover. Every evening before going on duty we were provided with an egg and a tin of soup to sustain us during the night! Day-time food was, I have to say, excellent.

At this time, female nurses were only allowed to work on the above-mentioned wards – I think the Navy must have thought it a little improper for the young ladies to go on some of the wards, even though the Sisters were female. I recall the 'killick' in charge of B2 didn't even like me to enter the sluice room.

Highlights were getting one's own room, lots of social functions, tennis on both Haslar and Dolphin's courts, and walking along the sea wall in the evenings with friends, where we sang and one of the boys played the banjo and one the cornet. In the summer a raft was moored a few yards out to sea so we had the chance to swim, which we did in very cold waters.

The other rather lovely thing that happened to me was when I selected as one of 12 nurses to attend the Cenotaph ceremony. We all had to go to HMS *Excellent* on Whale Island to learn how to march in step. Unlike the WRNS, the nurses at the time did not have to march or salute.

I finally left Haslar in August 1962 having been drafted to Malta.

Pauline Daniels (née Robson)

Patently good ideas

I started work at in 1961 as a blacksmith, which is a title dating back to the days of horse-drawn ambulances. The stables under A block can still be seen with their wooden block floor.

I really enjoyed my work; it was very varied, looking after all the different types of beds, Stryker frames (beds for traction) wheelchairs, and ward equipment like drug cupboards and trolleys.

I also had the chance to try out new ideas, working in conjunction with the doctors. In my time at Haslar I made five pieces of equipment on which the Admiralty took out a patent. It was good to see them being used on patients in the wards, such as a device to keep a patients head still, and nursing equipment to help nurses turn patients. I was awarded the British Empire Medal and Imperial Service Medal for my work within the hospital.

Bob Hillier and Superintending Nursing Sister Tricia Hambling with Guide Dog trophies representing the funds raised

I was invited by Matron and Sister Hamblyn to start fund-raising events for the Guide Dogs for the Blind, which then started the Haslar Fetes. I decided to walk from Trafalgar Square in London back to Gosport to open the Haslar Fete, which I did on five or six occasions. It was a non-stop walk that started at midday on Friday and got back around 2pm on Saturday. On the first walk, six people started out, but just myself and Roy Howard got back.

On the 60th Anniversary of D Day, we had some Canadian visitors in the hospital, and I was asked if I would like to show them round the underground Operating Theatres, used during the war, also the post-operative wards, as I was familiar with the undercroft and the cellars. Then I took them over to the Canada Block for tea and cake and a look round. It was a great honour to meet them. The women of Canada had paid for Canada Block in gratitude for the care give to the Canadian wounded.

I served in Haslar for 32 years and enjoyed every day, and was deeply saddened when they closed it.

Bob Hillier

Secret sleepers

During our recent Principal Training School 14 reunion we were reminiscing about the cupboard in G Block. The room opposite the galley on the ground floor had a big walk-in cupboard, and in it was yet another cupboard. This is where we hid and slept the night while we were on leave from other bases and visiting friends. Nurse Forsyth must have known what we were doing but she never said a word.

Lyn Howard

Much loved: Flossie Forsyth

My heavy bags

It was always a rush on a Friday afternoon to get down to the pontoon to catch a ferry over to Portsmouth. One particular Friday I had two large bags as I was taking things home to store, including books. I left the Annexe and stopped to rest my arms outside St Luke's when Surgeon Captain Milton-Thompson stopped and said "those bags look heavy – let me carry them for you". I tried to decline but he picked them up. From the look on his face during the slow walk down to the Archway, I think he wished he had not offered. I was sure the Matron would spot me and tell me off for allowing a Surgeon Captain to carry a rating's bag. I was so relieved when he gave them back to me in the Archway. After thanking him – and looking around to see who may have seen such a gesture – I scuttled away, managing to catch the ferry by the skin of my teeth.

Hilary Butterworth

Don't swear at me!

We had a hospital porter at Haslar called Trevor Mucket who, while on A3 ward, had an argument with the Nursing Sister in charge.

"What's your name?" she demanded.

"Mucket," he said.

The Sister reported him for swearing.

Mark Chapman

Still terrified

I remember … the Saturday night 'Chinky run' on night duty, Matron's rounds (I'm still terrified to this day), and taking an (occupied) bier over to the mortuary at 3am the night after watching Halloween.

Sue Harvey

The Haslar cat

I'd always wanted a cedar tree in my garden and at last my dream came true when we moved into the big house (or the 'Ad-Pad' as we called it) in 1980. My husband John was the Surgeon Rear Admiral in charge of naval hospitals and my job was to be in charge of entertainment on a grand scale.

One day, as we stood on the drawing-room balcony sipping an after-lunch coffee, one of our guests said "Do you realise you've a cat in the cedar tree?' and sure enough it was, a big ginger cat, about 10 or 12 feet up on one of the lowest branches.

As it was still there hours later, we planned its rescue:

1) Ladders for sailors to climb – too dangerous, apparently

2) RSPCA, even more amazingly, too dangerous.

3) Long ladder for 6ft 5in son Johnny, plus a long salmon fishing net. He tried, but the cat just ran up higher and higher.

It stayed in the tree, refusing all coaxing and offers of food and even survived a stormy night with heavy rain. (Did it drink rain from the little hollows in the bark, we wondered?).

After 19 days, it tried to climb down, head first, and literally fell out of the tree. I picked it up, took it to our garden shed and gave it a bowl of milk, which it slurped down in big noisy gulps – no gentle lapping now!

We were off the next day to our cottage in Devon, just for one night, so we left our ginger friend in the shed with lots of food and drink and when we returned he seemed quite fully restored, so we let him go, and we never saw him again. I often wondered what his owners thought when he turned up after three weeks missing!

A sad postscript: the cedar tree came down in the big storm of 1987.

Another note on the garden – about one and a half acres of it. When we took it over in 1980 there were no gardeners available. Tall sow thistles grew by the front door, and the roses, in beds shaped like an anchor, took me over four hours just to dead-head. John brought up our own mower from Devon and did all the grass cutting himself and we both worked hard for two years to restore the garden's original beauty.

It was sad to learn that after John retired in 1982 the garden became neglected again.

Elizabeth Haughton

Proud to have served

I was from a small Welsh town yet when I walked through those front gates for the first time, I just thought "I want to be here forever". I remember meeting my amazing classmates from Principal Training School 13. Haslar had a way of welcoming everyone, staff and patients alike, and I am proud to have served there.

Sandy Williams

The ladies were getting restless

While on night duty in the Receiving Room in 1970 or 1971 I took a telephone call in the early hours of the morning from House 11 or 12 (nurses residence) stating that they had water leaking through the ceiling. I called the duty plumber and he attended. Within half an hour a nurse telephoned again – the leak was persisting.

I went over and was met by at least a dozen young ladies scantily dressed in negligees and pyjamas – no wonder the plumber didn't wish to return!

The water was indeed still leaking down the central light fitting in one of the bedrooms. I had no idea where the stopcock was but I had to do something as these ladies were getting restless. So

Stephen Davies pictured on F5 ward in June 1968, when he was a Medical Assistant

was I, as I had some difficulty focusing on the leak.

I solved the problem temporarily by ripping the wooden pelmet from above the curtain rail and, using it as a trough, I secured one end of the light cord and directed the other end into the wash basin. Then I scarpered.

I never heard anything more about the leak or my vandalism of the pelmet.

Stephen Davies

Leave it to Sparks!

I was fortunate to get a job at Haslar as a hospital electrician at the age of 55, after leaving the army back in 1972 after 22 years of service as a radio technician in the Royal Signals and having many jobs over the ensuing years. I was interviewed for the Haslar job by a Naval Captain in charge of the works department. I had brought along several references from other jobs, and my Army ones, and was then asked what I knew about battery charging, to which I replied I had run a battery charging shop over in Cyprus when I was once stationed there. After the interview was over the Captain then informed me I could start work the following Monday.

I was introduced to the other artisans – Robby the blacksmith, Reg the carpenter and Bob the general labourer – and soon fitted in with them all. As it was near Christmas, I was tasked with checking and fixing all the Christmas lights for all the wards and sorting out those that were beyond repair. Each day we were told by the works department what jobs needed doing around the hospital and I was given works tickets for where fluorescent lights needed changing throughout the wards and remainder of the hospital: over a period of 10 years or more I must have replaced about 10,000 bedside lamps in the wards.

I got to know every part of the hospital with the cellars and attics, and the officers' and nurses' quarters. In between changing lights I did electrical checks on the personal electrical items belonging to the Nursing staff and the Officers' mess.

There was one room down in the cellars which was quite spooky, as it had rows and rows of large jars containing various parts of the human body, all preserved in a liquid called formaldehyde. One jar had a pair of Siamese twins in it, joined at the head: in earlier periods of the hospital there would not have been the expertise to separate them. Many of the jars would have been from Lord Nelson's era, and in those days surgeons would have used the remains as samples to teach the doctors.

In the summer months the Officers' Mess held a big event in a large marquee; I had to provide lots of coloured lights and extension leads for power for a band and any other unit requiring it. All the artisans were involved in setting up these events as the Naval other Ranks also had their own events requiring similar set ups with buffets and beer tents.

Then each Christmas I adorned the trees in front of the hospital with coloured chains of lights, and the carpenter and blacksmith and general labourer all worked on Santa's sleigh and reindeers. It looked lovely and the lights were set to come on once it started to get dark, so it was quite eye-catching.

During my years at Haslar I saw some of the older wards being completely gutted and refurbished to bring them more up to date at a cost of £2 million or more; one of the top older wards was made into a complete burns unit – yet when it was completed there weren't the staff to run it, which was a fiasco. When the Falklands was invaded by the

Argentinians, two empty wards were fully equipped with new beds and bedside lockers in the belief that there would be so many casualties coming there from that conflict, yet after all that preparation the wards never got used.

I used to cycle to work most days along the old railway line which was made into cycle paths and over Pneumonia Bridge, which was so named because in the winter months it was bitterly cold crossing over it. I had to be there for 7.30am but never had to clock on officially.

During my daily tasks around the hospital, I used a trolley where I could put a selection of lights and my stepladder and must have walked a fair old distance each day, but what with climbing up and down ladders and cycling to work and back, that was when I was my fittest.

Then there came a time when Robby retired and his job was taken over by a new chap called Ken, who was called on to do some lovely ornate ironwork for the church: he did a superb job, much admired by all who entered there.

I finally retired in January 2000, after over 10 happy years at Haslar and had a lovely send-off from all the works staff and fellow artisans. They had made a special cake with a little figure of me on top pushing my little trolley around. After I had retired, I heard Reg had too, and had emigrated to Australia. Sadly he died from cancer and a few years later Ken, who was a lot younger than us all, died of a heart attack, with Bob following him a year or two later.

Brian Furlong

A traumatic death

As a nurse for 40 years I have inevitably been present at many deaths, some peaceful and others traumatic. However, while working as a Staff Nurse on Acute Medical Receiving I witnessed a death that has remained vivid, as no-one present that day was able to help. The male patient had been admitted after a heart attack and his mind had reverted back to the terrible experiences that he had been subjected to during the war. He had been held captive in a German Concentration Camp and his wife explained the torture he had experienced was at the hands of female German concentration camp officers.

This acute condition resulted in the poor man being absolutely petrified of all the nurses. Apparently, after the war he was sent to a hospital staffed by male orderlies who wore white coats and on the first day of his admission to Haslar one of the Medical Assistants put a white coat on and was able to get near him for a short while. However, that evening he sustained a second heart attack and he cowered up the corner in fright, not allowing me or anyone else near him, and that is where he died. Post-Traumatic Stress Disorder was not really appreciated in those days and it made me realise that, as young nurses, we had no idea what people really went through during war and conflict.

Hilary Butterworth

New beds but no patients

I believe we were the last people to work in Haslar and had to install new radiators and covers in wards by a certain date, due to closure. As we were finishing, we were hampered by trucks and technicians installing specialist German beds. These beds would allow for critical examination, X-rays, scans etc to be done without moving the injured patients, which otherwise is a big problem. Staff told us the total scheme cost in the order of a million pounds. I think there were 20 beds in the ward we worked on. Staff had to be specially trained to work them – but they were never used.

Howard Staniforth

Storm caused mayhem

In later years Haslar was proud of its best-cleaned hospital awards but back in the 1960s cleaning was undertaken by the staff as opposed to civilian cleaners. Some of the wards still had teak floors and had to be swept and polished using block bumpers on long handles swung back and forth. Some short cuts were tried including using a woollen blanket with a member of staff sitting inside, but sometimes splinters caused shouts of pain and it was back to the bumper again.

Some wards had terrazzo floors (smooth marble chips); it was normal on Fridays to deep clean. Beds were pushed to one side with patients watching proceedings from their beds as staff swept, having laid down tea leaves to absorb the dirt. Some lads even took their shoes and socks off and rolled up their bell-bottom trousers as they mopped. Once the floor was dry the routine was repeated, having pushed all the beds back to the other side.

In summer months and in fine weather, patients were taken down to the Quadrangle on their beds, with a supply of juice and water, along with bottles of stout for male patients. This was always enjoyed by patients and visitors, but one summer's day all turned to mayhem when a storm broke with some 20+ beds in the Quadrangle. Staff could not move patients that quickly, with slow lifts that had room for only one bed at a time. This resulted in patients and beds becoming soaked and the last few beds and mattresses sodden with the rain.

We were told that during World War II patients were moved into the cellars and air-raid shelters. Patients with major fractures who had framed beds were too bulky to be moved and stayed put in the ward. The patient was left with a carafe of water, a bottle and the top of the bed covered by a second mattress in case of the ceiling falling in.

One ward routine that was always keenly awaited by patients was the evening drinks round – tea, coffee, chocolate and Brickwood's beer delivered daily by Brickwood's to the victualling office. I personally noted a Doctor also writing a prescription for a bottle of whisky for an alcoholic patient.

The same doctor also admitted a local undertaker for surgery, but the patient in question – grey haired and with a long face – just sat and looked up and down the ward and appeared to measure up each patient for their wooden suit. Surgeon Commander Peter Bond went to the changing room and removed a long mirror and placed it on a chair in front of the patient and told him to measure himself, much to the amusement of all.

Eric Birbeck

In love since the Great War

Haslar was home to many love stories, but one wonderful couple in love has always remained clear in my memory.

The 80-year-old male patient was confined to his bed on intravenous fluids. Although he and his wife lived locally, due to her inability to climb the stairs she had been unable to visit him. He was clearly missing her and I arranged to meet her from a taxi at visiting time with a wheelchair and bring her up the lift.

As I was wheeling her to his bed, he spotted her coming and was so excited, frantically trying to sit up to reach her. The beds in those days could not be lowered but I was able to get the large cumbersome wheelchair close enough so he could at least hold her hand.

At the end of visiting time he tried unsuccessfully to reach her for a kiss, so with the help of another nurse we stood her up and held her so he was able to kiss her. It was a lovely moment and both myself and the other nurse had tears in our eyes.

When I wheeled her back down in the lift to await the taxi I asked her how long they had been married. I was expecting her to say many years, but was surprised when she said just eight years, although they had been in love since they first met when she was 16 and he was 17 during the Great War. Her family had not approved of him and they had been forced to meet each other in France twice a year. They had not got married until the last of her brothers died eight years ago. It was so special to see the love they held for each other, but so sad they had lived separately all that time. I was so glad we had managed to get her in to Haslar that day.

Hilary Butterworth

Radio Haslar goes live

I spent 16 years of my life at Haslar – small in comparison to most other people, I guess, but I was proud to be associated with it. My association with the hospital is via Radio Haslar. Our studios were based next door in a three-storey house (we called it Radio House) in Fort Blockhouse, but broadcasting to patients around the wards. We provided over 60 hours of live local programming every week, featuring local news and sport but primarily requests and dedications from patients and staff.

The journey for me started in 1991, with setting up the idea of hospital radio there; over a two-year period there were endless meetings and negotiations with management of Haslar. We established the service, launching on 14 March 1993. Even though I was chairman from the start, as well as programme controller for most of those 16 years and presenting other programmes, the best bit was walking the wards. I enjoyed meeting the patients and sharing music memories as well as listening to their stories, which made it far more interesting than just presenting a music request programme. I also liked being part of the various Haslar fetes: we broadcast live back to the wards from within the grounds. Then there were the annual Christmas Carol concerts from St Luke's Church.

I will never ever forget Haslar and when the time came to cease broadcasting there and move the station to new studios at Bury House (within the Thorngate Halls) it was the biggest wrench in my life. However, in 2012 I decided to call it a day and joined Portsmouth's Express FM. I may be at another station now, but I am proud of the contribution and the achievements that our Radio Haslar team made.

Chris Pearce

Stay in your seats, girls!

I first trained as a Probationary Medical Technician (Physio), commencing my specialist training at the Royal Naval School of Physiotherapy in September 1973.

I recall that sometime between then and my leaving the Physio school in December 1975, a Haslar Casualty Plan was declared: there had been a gas leak in the suture packing department at the local Cyanamid factory on Fareham Road, Gosport.

Haslar was inundated with numerous casualties, some of whom needed ward admission, but many just needing a precautionary checkup. I recall that the walking wounded were taken to the Physio Department's gymnasium where they were assessed. I had to perform a satisfactory Vitalograph – to measure their lung capacity – before they could be discharged.

I recall the proceedings starting in an orderly fashion. More and more women arrived, and were allocated a numbered seat, at which they needed to remain so that the physio staff could main a record of how everyone was doing. But things started to go wrong when they saw their friends on the opposite side of the gym. Needless to say, the whole thing descended into near chaos because we lost track of who was supposed to be sitting where. It took some time to restore order and to get back on track.

Bob Beckwith

You're my sheet anchor

A memory that still can bring tears to my eyes after more than 40 years relates to the story of Mr J, an elderly patient on a men's medical ward in E block at Haslar in 1973. I was a blue belt (a second Year Nurse in training) and well into the second year of my SRN training as a proud member of QARNNS.

Mr J was admitted to the ward with what we know much more about nowadays, some form of dementia. He was probably in his seventies and he was not only distressed because he couldn't understand why he was in hospital, he was confused and sad. Like many people with dementia he had very limited short-term memory and would ask over and over again: "Where am I? What am I doing here? Where is my wife?" He would ask these questions repeatedly to everyone and anyone that walked past his bed, dozens of times a day.

I can see him now: his bed was by the door to the sluice on one of the long Nightingale wards in the old E block. He was a lean man of about 5'10" and I think had probably been a good-looking chap in his day. I became very fond Mr J and seemed to have the time to talk with him, something that seems to be a luxury in nursing today. He told me he had been a Yeoman Signaller in the war and did I know what that was? "No," said I, so he told me all about what he did in the war.

Maybe it was because I enjoyed talking and I was interested in the war that he remembered me, so much so that he called me 'his sheet anchor' … Did I know what that was? "No," said I, so he told me that it was the last anchor – the one you rely on in a storm or when things are bad. And for several weeks we had the same conversation every day several times. He stopped being anxious and seemed less distressed when his wife left after visiting time.

Mr J was discharged and later that year I was drafted with my class to Stonehouse for our third year. About halfway through our purple belt year (the third year of State Registered Nurse in training), at Easter, I was taken ill with pneumonia and admitted as an inpatient to the Sick Officers Block with a lovely single room, and a gin-and-orange when fit enough. I was quite poorly and had to have penicillin injections four times a day. A night nurse who came in with the jab was a qualified SEN just drafted from Haslar and she saw my name.

"That's odd," she said. "I had a patient at Haslar who kept asking for somebody called Nurse Cox and we couldn't find anyone with that name. We couldn't placate him – he kept saying 'if you find Nurse Cox I will be OK as she is my sheet anchor'."

And of course it was my Mr J. Can you imagine how I felt? However ridiculous it was, I just wanted to get out of my bed and find him; I was so upset.

Of course I never got to see him again and never knew what happened to him, but I hope he found another sheet anchor. Although it's a sad story it makes me remember why I became a nurse, why I am proud of my training as a Naval Nurse and why nursing is so special … because we make a difference. And sometimes we can be a sheet anchor.

Bobbie Johnson (née Cox)

Superintending Nursing Sister Cathy Greenslade (née Tunnicliff) poses for a recruiting photo with QARNNS colleagues

Chapter Three
Praise and Worship – St Luke's and St Mary's

St Luke's was built in 1762 as an afterthought by the Admiralty. Originally a chapel was meant to be included in the 'fourth side' of Haslar as part of the original design. An overrun of the original budget for the hospital caused the fourth side not to be built and therefore there was no chapel. Records show that services were held in the Food Hall from 1753 and for a time there were plans to have a chapel over the hospital Arcade.

On completion of Haslar, application was made for funding to build a separate chapel and though this was granted, the budget was very tight – in fact one Admiralty letter stipulated that no funds would be available beyond that offered.

St Luke's was built and became the centre of the hospital until it was forced to close briefly in 1963: death-watch beetle had ruined the roof and there were no funds available for repair. Eventually the work was undertaken by the dockyard and at times overseen by the Georgian Society, led by Sir John Betjeman. St Luke's was re-dedicated in October 1964.

It was in St Luke's in 2002 that Haslar staff first learnt of the planned closure of the hospital. The chapel itself was closed in March 2007.

On closure, the Ministry of Defence disposed of many items from St Luke's, some of which Haslar Heritage Group managed to regain. They also arranged a loan of the silver from the Royal Navy Trophy Store. The base of the cross on the altar is made from a section of sixteenth century ship's timber taken from the ceiling of the old C Block. The base is surmounted by a new oak cross, signifying new rising from the old, and is dedicated to all who served at Haslar. It was made by Commander Ken Enticknap. The new memorial cross of fused French vanilla and copper glass, encased in a copper case, was made to replace the earlier chrome cross – which was given to a Naval chapel - and was presented by Eric Birbeck.

Through the efforts of Haslar Heritage Group and with the approval of the new owners of Haslar, St Luke's was once again opened for services on a monthly basis in 2010 and has acted as the Group's centre since then.

It was re-dedicated in October 2012 by the Bishop of Portsmouth and the then chaplain of the Fleet and since held services, funerals, baptisms and wedding blessings.

Haslar also had its own Roman Catholic Chapel. St Mary's stood within the structure between 'C' and 'D' blocks and was built after the bombing of the Haslar Museum in October 1941. It was in existence until 1980, when it was demolished to make way for the Crosslink building. At this point a small room was made available on the first floor of the main Arcade of the hospital for services and reflection.

The Bishop of Portsmouth and Chaplain of the Fleet with
the Rev Philip Hiscock (right), vicar of St Luke's
Re-dedication of St Luke's 2012

Clergy of St Luke's from 1946 with their date of appointment

Cyril Owen Amos Darby	June 1946
Perry Malby Dodwell	September 1949
Charles Patrick de Candole	July 1953
Cuthbert Guy Desormeaux Long	November 1955
John Stanton Jeans	January 1958
Julian James Andrew Newman	September 1960
Evelyn Hugh Jenoyr Levinge	October 1964
Martin Kitchener Orme	March 1967
David Vincent Evans	January 1970
Leslie John De Groose	October 1971
Peter Woodhall	January 1974
Anthony Arthur Upton	March 1976
Peter John Gregson	May 1976
John Edmund Frank Rawlings	December 1978
John Edward Goodband Clark	June 1981
Anthony John Francis Metters	August 1982
Richard Francis Buckley	January 1985
Michael John Smith	September 1987
Stephen Philip Pickering	May 1990
Steven David Brookes	August 1992
David Barlow	
Christopher John Luckcraft	
Jeremy Peter Ames	
John Hill *(last Naval Chaplain)*	October 2004
Military withdrawal from Royal Hospital Haslar	March 2007
Reverend Canon Edward Goodyer	October 2010
Reverend Philip Hiscock	June 2012

The choir pictured in 1957

Hymn singing in the wards

After evening service on Sundays, the choir from St Luke's would visit two wards of the hospital and sing hymn requests, working our way around the hospital over a period of time. At some of the wards the patients would give us models of boats or planes they had made as part of their physiotherapy. These visits included the psychiatric unit overlooking the sea wall: for a boy of 12 this was quite an ordeal and somewhat alarming. At Christmas we would sing around the wards over the week before Christmas Eve. After each night we were served with a buffet supper by the leading departments of the hospital, ending the week at the admiral's residence.

Friday nights was choir practice, ending up with snooker or table tennis at the Errol Hall near the now Main Gate. In the summer it was cricket at the sports field at HMS *Dolphin*. As a treat one year we had a trip around the Isle of Wight onboard a Motor Torpedo Boat from HMS *Hornet*, which as great fun. I remained in the choir until the age of 16 and was Head Chorister.

Tony Pearce

A little worse for wear

I joined Haslar from HMS *Collingwood* in early January 1960 as a Probationary Sick Berth Attendant. As trainees we were billeted over the road at HMS *Dolphin*. We had some great and very happy times there. Our commanding officer at Haslar was Surgeon Vice Admiral Sir Derek Steel Perkins, who was also medical officer to the Royal Yacht Britannia when she sailed with the Queen on board.

One of my lasting memories is of the Admiral's eldest daughter getting married in

St Luke's and his youngest daughter going missing during the reception. She was eventually found by a search party, sound asleep on the stairs in the Infectious Disease unit, a little worse for wear. All the staff were treated to a drink to celebrate the wedding and the finding of the youngest daughter.

I made a lot of good friends at Haslar and was sorry to leave for a new posting, which was to the marine depot in Deal in 1961. Two of those friends followed me to Deal and on to the naval hospital in Malta.

John Roffey

Chocolate was a treat

I have great memories of Haslar, especially of St Luke's. As a child I attended Sunday School. Mr Evans was our Sunday School teacher. I loved the outings we went on, to places like Portchester Castle and Hayling Island.

When I reached the age of twelve in 1951, my friend Vivien Healy and I were asked if we would like to become members of the church choir. It was choir practice every Friday evening and church twice on Sunday. We loved being a part of the hospital choir and after evensong we would all go along to the hospital wards with the portable organ and sing hymns requested by the patients. We were often given chocolate by the patients – that was a real treat.

On Friday evenings after choir practice we all went into the Errol Hall for recreation.

The choir pictured in 1953 or 1954. Betty Archer is second from the right in the top row and Vivien Healy is next to her on the end. Mr Evans, the Sunday School teacher, is to the right of the Naval officer

On one occasion, the small piano on the stage was knocked over and my foot was in the way. So I was the one who ended up in the hospital. Luckily there was no lasting damage and I got a ride home in the vicar's car. I left the choir when I was sixteen. They were happy days and I still sing in a choir now at the age of seventy-eight.

Betty Archer

A major part in my life

I sang in the choir at St Luke's and my favourite memories are singing on the wards before Midnight Mass on Christmas Eve.

St Luke's has played a major part in my life over the years. My sister Kathrin Latimer was married there. My father, Ian Latimer, was the first Lieutenant of Haslar and two years ago his memorial service was held here.

Jacky Broadbent

Such a special place

I was born and bred in Gosport and my main memory of Haslar is being married in the beautiful little church of St Lukes in 1971. It is such a special place. The nurses came out with patients in wheelchairs to watch us leave the church.

Also the great care my whole family received when being treated at various times, as both in-patients and out-patients.

Marian Lee

Del et pinxit

In 2009 I started to research the background to St Luke's and especially its refurbishment in 1963/4 when the roof was ravaged by Death Watch beetle.

For many years I had attempted to research the background to the stained glass and who was responsible for its production and original installation. The windows are memorial windows to patients who died in Haslar and to Medical Officers killed on active service.

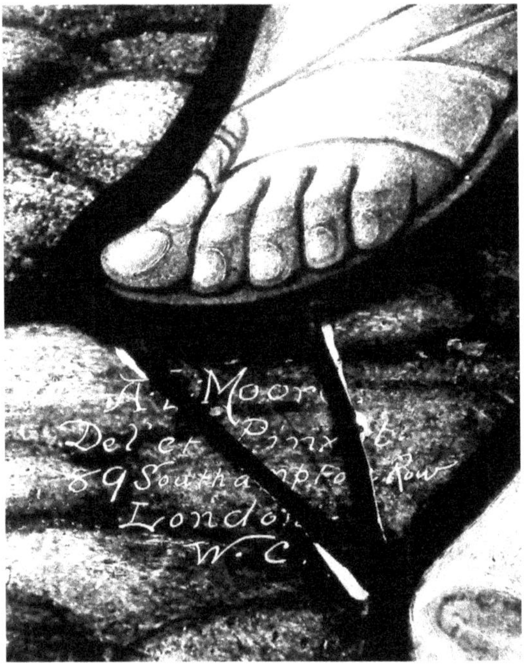

All prayers seem to be answered and I am grateful to a man who attended St Luke's one afternoon in 2012 during Heritage Days. I had noticed a very slight gentleman sitting in the middle of the pews and – unusually – he still had his hat on. He was looking at the stained glass windows with a small pair of binoculars.

I approached him and introduced myself. I explained my part in Haslar

Heritage and my wish to know just who was responsible for the stained glass windows. He smiled at me and rose from the pew and walked me to the first window by the pulpit and instructed me to follow a line of sight above the inscription, by the depiction of Christ's sandal … there in a small piece of glass was a signature: 'AL Moore London WC' and 'Del et Pinxit', meaning 'he drew and painted'. The same was found on the facing stained glass window. I turned to thank the gentleman but he had completely vanished. Although for me a question had been answered, the event had left me somewhat chilled and wondering who the man could have been. Was it possibly AL Moore in spirit, checking his work?

Eric Birbeck

Eightpence a week for choirboys

I was a choirboy at St Luke's Church from October 1954 for approximately two years. I lived in Tamworth Place off Alver Road, near Workhouse Lake. I joined the choir with other local boys and girls from the area. De Candole was the vicar and Mr Evans was the verger.

Choir practice was on Friday evenings and after this we would play various games in Errol Hall. There was a Sunday morning service – the last hymn was always 'For Those in Peril on the Sea' – and an evening one. This was then followed by the choir singing in two of the hospital wards, and we were always being told off for running between wards in our surplices. This was four engagements in all, for which we received eightpence (2d for each engagement). We had to wait 13 weeks to be paid, though! On one evening service, there was only one person in the congregation, but we still sang.

There was a national railway strike in 1955 and I am ashamed to say some of us boys copied this one Sunday evening. We still attended church but sat at the back. Not one of my better moments.

The choir outing of 1955 was to Carisbrooke Castle. We went from HMS *Hornet* by Motor Torpedo Boat (all of us out on deck) to Cowes, then by train to Newport. Questions would be asked in the House of Commons today about the cost of fuel and a naval vessel for just 12 boys and girls.

St Luke's did not have toilets, but the choirboys would use the boiler room under the east end, peeing against the boiler. A sauna with a difference!
I was a patient in Haslar Hospital in 1989 for an operation on my varicose veins. My treatment was first class, as was the cleanliness and care I received.

Bob Harrop

Some of the choir on the outing to Carisbrooke Castle in 1955

Great skill of hand

My good friend Ken Ball was a welder who worked in Haslar mending broken equipment and beds, but he also created much of the wrought-iron work and hand rails that you see in St Luke's Church. Ken tragically passed away very young some years ago. I hope his wife Maggie will see this and commemorate his great skill of hand. I am sure it would be something his two daughters would love to see him remembered for. He was a good man.

For myself, I would like to thank Haslar for taking great care of my wife when she underwent spinal surgery. She has never looked back. And for all of the times that I drove my two sons to A&E with various cuts and breaks over their youth.

Guy Nicholls

A wedding at St Luke's

My father worked at Haslar after the Second World War and left with the rank of Wardmaster Lieutenant Commander. I was married in 1971 at St Luke's Church and the reception was held in the Medical Mess. My mother sadly passed away at Haslar in 1988.

Veronica Phillips

A true artisan

My late husband was called Ken Ball. He worked as a blacksmith and artisan at Haslar for 10 years from 1993 to 2003. He passed away in November 2003 aged 46. He did an apprenticeship at the Dockyard and also worked at Frater and Fleetlands. He also worked at DERA (the Defence Research Establishment) for a few years, across the road from Haslar. He could turn his hand to anything from fixing beds to doing the wrought-ironwork in St Luke's church.

Margaret Ball

Raising the roof: VE Day

By the outbreak of World War II in September 1939, Haslar had served the Royal Navy for 186 years and already taken its rightful place in history. Through the years of that new war, Haslar's staff would once again be tested in caring for the sick and injured in conflict: patients had always been treated the same, whether they were friend or foe, from Trafalgar and Crimea through to the Great War.

Tuesday 8 May 1945 – Victory in Europe Day – was a normal working day at Haslar. Patients were cared for on busy wards and staff in the cellar Operating Theatres carried on as normal preparing for operations; even making tea from the boiling water from a spare steriliser, and eating NAAFI biscuits between operations. The change meant no 'blackout' at night and no more need to transfer able patients to the air raid shelters in the basements. Throughout the war those incapable of being moved – especially those with fractures and on traction – remained in the wards to brave the raids, but there were no record of injuries.

Helen Long, a VAD nurse who worked in the underground Theatres, described her time there in her book 'Change into Uniform':

“There were two Operating Theatres with three operating tables in each Theatre, each table staffed by a surgical team – a surgeon, anaesthetist, and nursing assistants. The corridors and stairs were in darkness to save electricity and staff could only use the lift if they accompanied a patient. There was the ever-present smell of gas gangrene in the air, something that all VADs who worked in the Operating Theatres mentioned when questioned: the smell arose because many gangrenous limbs were stored until the pressure of work had subsided and staff could deal with their disposal. VADs state that their Commandant, Miss I M Wastell, sent her girls up for some fresh sea air when time permitted as the war drew to a close.

Phyllis Pearson, a VAD who worked in Operating Theatres, recalled her most vivid memory was that of a severely wounded Canadian soldier. Just before he was to go into Theatre he muttered: ‘Be an angel and get me a drink’. As he couldn’t have anything by mouth, Phyllis wrung out a gauze swab and held it to his lips. He gave a sigh. ‘You’re an angel!’ he said. Those were his last words as he did not survive surgery.

To reach theatre we had to go down the staircase in the centre block and walk through dimly lit cellars. One day our first case was an amputation of a gangrenous leg. Whilst having a coffee break before the next case, the Surgeon Commander asked if I was alright.

‘Yes thank you,’ I replied.

He pursued the question again and I finally said:

‘Well if you must know as I was coming through the cellars I passed three dead mice,’ and I promptly burst into tears!

When I came off duty I showered and slept for four hours and went to the galley and there were strawberries – a welcome treat. However, the smell of ether and gangrene in our clothes stayed with me and since that day I have never been able to eat a strawberry. Even seeing them on roadside stalls these days brings home the smell of the Theatres back to me.

During the war Haslar had dealt with some 83,446 patients, especially during the Dunkirk evacuation and on D Day, when Haslar was in direct receipt of casualties from the Normandy beachheads. The underground Operating Theatres were the brainchild of Surgeon Rear Admiral Cecil Wakely in conjunction with a surgical team including Brigadier Elliot Cutler of the US Army: their combined planning was to save many lives.

During the war, staff worked alongside Nursing Sisters of QARNNS (the Queen Alexandra’s Royal Naval Nursing Service), Sick Berth staff and VADs (Voluntary Aid Detachment), with members of the Medical Branch naval reserve, all in support of Royal Naval Medical and Dental Officers. In turn, these were supported by a civil service staff and members of the Red Cross and St John’s. Over 3,000 Royal Navy Sick Berth Branch Probationers were trained at Haslar, the busiest year being 1941 when 827 were trained. Almost 600 Royal Naval medical branch personnel including QARNNS and VAD nurses lost their lives during the war.

Haslar was touched by air raids and fires caused by incendiaries during air raids that were directed mainly at Portsmouth, especially at the Dockyard and depots. It was always said that Haslar was spared thanks to the water tower being of use to the German Luftwaffe as a direction finder, and the large red cross on a white background placed on the lawn of the hospital quadrangle.

Staff tell of German prisoners-of-war who needed surgery screaming on their way to the Operating Theatres, as they had been told by their superiors that if captured and requiring treatment the enemy (us) would not give them an anaesthetic for surgery. Others were charming having been educated at either Oxford or Cambridge.

During one air raid in 1941 the Haslar Museum received a direct hit and sadly many books and specimens from the founding of the museum in the 1830s were destroyed. In the spring of 1941 a direct hit on the medical store caused the loss of £80,000-worth of medical supplies.

In 1941, through Haslar, the first Royal Naval Blood Transfusion unit had been formed and this in turn saved many lives.

Among the patients there was also a ship's cat. In 1940 HMS *Worcester* was damaged by a bomb attack while on Channel escort and patrol duties; some 40 injured of the ship's crew were transferred to Haslar for treatment. They all arrived at the Casualty reception and the last sailor was carrying Worcester, the ship's cat. He had been injured in the hind leg by a splinter and the admitting surgeon was told that if Worcester was not treated, then all the sailors would leave! Needless to say Worcester was admitted and he went to Theatre (last) and had his leg treated and bandaged. One of the VADs present described the cat on a stretcher lying on his back, with his fully bandaged leg in the air. He was admitted to the ward along with his shipmates and slept in an orange box. A few days later when the surgeon came to carry out his ward round, Worcester accompanied him as he visited every one of Worcester's shipmates. They were all discharged and Worcester was never heard of again.

On VE night throughout Gosport, Portsmouth and across the nation, there were crowds everywhere, and people dancing round bonfires in the streets. It was of course, the night when the lights came on again all over the country. The ships in Portsmouth Harbour made the air victoriously hideous with their own peculiar kind of noise, and Haslar's solitary chapel bell of St Luke's rang madly – a combination which tightened my throat, filled my eyes, and made my knees turn to jelly, so much so that I had to sit down.

The chapel of St Luke's, its windows aglow and wonderfully innocent now of blackout, was suddenly to become, by common consent, the focal point. The Quarter-deck (Quadrangle) and all roads and footpaths leading to the little church began to fill with patients and staff.

The service was short and to the point, as we roared our praise and thanksgiving until we all but raised the roof, ending with 'O God, Our help in ages past' and the National Anthem. As the men retrieved their fore-and-aft and square-rig caps, eyes were brimming over, and face grey with late night fatigue and great weariness of soul smiled.

We all trooped out into the merciful darkness, too moved to speak – reluctant even, some of us, to leave this hallowed place, where it was easiest to keep contact with our dead. Tightly cocooned in my scarlet-lined cape, I lingered in the edge of the shrubbery until everyone had gone, and made a secret pact with myself to try to remember them all, as I walked – oh so slowly – the length of the now deserted Quarter-deck. The dead of Dunkirk, of that daring raid on St Nazaire; the men who now lay in the desert sands, the men of the Malta convoys and the men on the Normandy beaches.

Helen Long

Extracted from 'Change into Uniform' by Helen Long (née Vlasto) with permission of the publishers, Terence Dalton Ltd

St Luke's prior to refurbishment in 1964

A photograph from the Edwardian period, with the ivy-clad St Luke's overlooking the hospital quadrangle

A 'Holy Joe'

I joined Haslar training division in 1972 as Junior Medical Assistant 2nd Class. On Sunday morning I was getting into my best Naval suit – my No. 1s – ready to go to St Mary's Roman Catholic church at Haslar. One of my mess mates said he hadn't had me down as a 'Holy Joe'. I asked what they would be doing for the next few hours, to which they replied: "Sunday morning cleaning duties."

I pointed out that I was going to listen to a story, have a sing-song, eat a piece of thin bread, and drink a swig of wine. I converted eight of them to Catholics for the next Sunday.

John (Scouse) Redmond

Laughter at Midnight Mass

I remember going to a Christmas Midnight Mass with Mary Stafford, where we thought we might get thrown out! We were biting into our capes so to stop the hysterical laughing after we saw the priest's open-toed plaster cast peeping out from underneath his vestments! Why it made us laugh so much I don't know. It certainly made us forget being homesick.

Jane Hahn (née Baker)

Full circle

My late wife Anne and I were both serving in Haslar and were married in St Mary's in March 1976. I had recently completed my Medical Assistant's training and Anne was in R Class. The best man decided that he would put the rings somewhere safe (on his finger), but on the way to the church realised he couldn't get them off. The priest,

Father John Beecher (RIP) – always one to see the funny side – offered a solution: if we rushed we could still get to Fratton Park for the first half! The three of us together with the organist frantically tried everything to get the rings off and five minutes before the bride arrived we succeeded.

The story comes full circle nearly 30 years later when, in November 2005, Anne died suddenly and unexpectedly. Two days before she died, she had been on F2, which in the 1970s was D Block (nurses accommodation) and just to the right of where St Mary's once was.

Nigel Hearnden

Every Sunday

I was in Principal Training School and joined in May 1969. I loved St Mary's Church and went to Mass there every Sunday. When I was on ward E3, there was a delightful Superintendent Sister – Mary Doyle – who was very insistent that I attend Mass and always made a point of organising the morning work accordingly. She sadly passed away in 2016 in Reading. She was an active member of the Thames Valley QARNNS group.

When I returned to Haslar from Plymouth for my staffing year on the Children's Ward (A6) I went on a pilgrimage to Lourdes with the little congregation of St Mary's church. The priest went on to become bishop to the Forces. It was a very happy time and we went to help the sick pilgrims attend the services at the grotto of Our Lady of Lourdes. I keep the photo in my Sunday Missal and often think about the privilege it was to go there as a Naval Nurse.

Sue Richards (née Price)

The pilgrimage to Lourdes with the priest pictured far right

Opposite page: St Mary's Catholic chapel. Above: Admiral's Walk and St Luke's, with the infamous puddle in the foreground

Christmas 1949

Chapter Four
Second To None – Stories From Patients

Royal Haslar opened to naval patients in 1753 and after a few rough years set the standard for patient care. Over the decades of the eighteenth and early nineteenth centuries this was also to include naval pensioners and the returning armies and navies of other countries, including Russia. Patient numbers increased throughout the years.

In 1948, with the inception of the National Health Service, 84 beds were made available for the treatment of local Gosport residents. Throughout the 1950s and 60s, more civilian patients and naval families were gradually included. During this time members of the other armed services were also treated at Haslar depending on where they were based.

During the 1950s and 60s, service patients – when admitted even for simple surgery such as the removal of an appendix, or treatment of a hernia – would stay for weeks, to include sick leave and return for final discharge. This was because many were drafted off their ships to Haslar and then discharged as fit to another ship or naval base.

A wide range of clinical care was available to patients, especially in later years: by the late 1990s there were seven modern operating theatres undertaking a variety of operations. In one six-month period at the turn of the millennium, 1,000 hip and knee replacements were carried out.

It is not easy to determine how many patients passed through Haslar's gates over the years, but one record of operations in the mid-1980s indicates that some 16,000 operations had taken place in a single year.

Changes in staffing took place in 1996 when many service hospitals had closed and Haslar became a tri-service hospital with at least another ten years of service to run. It was at this point that NHS staff from the Queen Alexandra hospital at Cosham started to work at Haslar: eventually they worked in all departments, especially in the last three years up to 2009 and closure.

What was very noticeable within a few months of NHS staff joining Haslar was that they absorbed the military ethos, even using military terms and smartened-up uniforms.

There is not a patient who does not have, or hold, fond memories of Haslar from across the years, as this chapter shows.

A welcome for the Bird Man

I heard mum going off to work ..."Don't forget to feed the cat" ... and I rolled out of bed and went downstairs to give Albert his saucer of milk and watch him clean the tin plate of fishy leftovers.

After a few painful steps I was feeling giddy. It was the last day of my 48-hour leave – and today I was due to return to the RAF. Painfully I just made the walk to the surgery at the end of our road. One look and the nurse called the doc … and he reached for the phone. All I heard was "an ambulance for Haslar."

Of course there was a great, long gap before the clouds left me. When I looked around, I was in bed. Alongside me a pint bottle of beer and a packet of fags. Later, the chap in the next bed offered me a cigarette. Then I went to sleep again.

The ward ran a long way: it had eight or nine tall windows, each with a bed alongside, and lying on the beds or sitting at chairs at the end sat matelots, some of them wearing naval rig. It wasn't long before they figured out I wasn't a sailor; one of them called to his mates "Welcome to the Bird Man" and the whole gang cheered.

Despite my fuzzy mind I tried to chat with the boys... but my next bed-mate said to his pals, "Let him drop off to sleep, you noisy lot. They will be round poking and pulling him about, like they did to us, remember?"

They all started in with disparaging views about the lob-lolly* boys. My pal in the next bed said to me: "Stiffen up, mate. Prepare yourself. They'll be round to see how the skin looks. So don't go picking at the bandage – that's fatal. You just don't try pulling the bandage off – you'll probably faint away. Just stick out your jaw and look the bugger in the eye. Then he'll remove the plaster with one quick pull. And believe us – we've all been there – that is going to sting more than anything you could have eased off yourself. Couple of days, you'll be the pride of the Royal Air Force. And you'll be as smart as any matelot in the fleet, eh?"

Next morning, a couple of lob-lolly boys (still what the medics were called and had been since Nelson's day*) marched in, led by a smart young medical officer.

"Stand easy," he said. " Feeling all right?"

"No pain, sir," I said.

"Let's have a look then." Then ZIP, away with the bandage, revealing a neatly sewn scar.

"Well done. We've taken that appendix out. We'll keep an eye on you for a while, but it looks fine. You'll be back flapping your wings in no time."

That afternoon my mother came to the ward. No surprise. She'd spent many a long day popping into Haslar – countless times to see my dad and to push him around in a wheelchair. Come to that, I used to push dad around Haslar before they fixed his arm and gave him a pretty good dockyard job. Turns out he had a gift for experimenting with different ways of making exciting grub for sub-mariners, to overcome the boring days under the sea.

A couple of the boys took me down to see the Haslar Shop, complete with duty-free fags and beers and – best of all – our teatime cakes that we relied on to top up. The boys swore they were even better than anything their mums used to make.

I got told off by one of the POs when I got up early and – armed with a wide broom – cleared the floor from end to end. Too good for him, my pals said.

Obviously I couldn't just wander around Haslar – even if the enemy had hidden my uniform away. And then one of our gang found me a reasonable all-in-one cookhouse worksuit. And one or other of us would nick a different cap, making a careful cover for the Bird Man.

One happy morning a soft voice stopped me: "Hello John. What are you doing here?"

Brenda was not only the girlfriend of one of my old school pals, she was one of

Haslar's office girls. She had a break in the afternoon and she showed me round, especially her favourite spot – looking through the trees at a vista of rolling waters, a bluey green you'd never see anywhere else on earth. With the long-lasting freshness in the air from the sea.

And then there was the entertainment: "There's a new film – from the States," said Taffy, and that's how after our teatime we went to the mess hall, now looking more like a music hall to get the biggest blasting from Bill Haley and his Comets with 'Rock around the Clock'. In a matter of days of release of the film, Britain's Teddy Boys and their Dolls went berserk, tearing up cinema seats to dance in the aisles, probably leaving Haslar the only undamaged theatre in the south of England.

One day a lob-lolly boy came to see Barry, one of my pals on the ward, and in his hands he carried a nasty set of handcuffs. A few of us were sitting around waiting for lunchtime.

"Come on," said the PO. "Let's just get it over with."

Then Barry smiled at him, leaned over and said "If you are going to take me across the water to Pompey, you will find that the regulations forbid the restraint of anyone being taken across water."

Collapse of Stout Party (as we used to say).

In stark contrast to the March of the Teddy Boys, the Haslar drama group offered us Noel Coward's 'Blithe Spirit', about the hysterical fate of a widowed young man about to marry his new love, while the ghost of the old one persists in making his life hell. (And how!) I never knew you could be so entertained in a busy hospital.

But at last my time was up and I report to the Captain of Haslar, as every leaving patient had to do.

"Ah, Able Seaman Bull," he said. "I've had a very strange signal about you. They want me to send you to HMS *Daedalus* at Lee-on-the-Solent, so they can send an aircraft from RAF Upavon to take you back. I can't possibly be party to sending Other Ranks flying about the country."

So I spent a day travelling back to Upavon, only to return home to Gosport almost immediately for a fortnight's leave.

John Bull

* *Loblolly boys were originally the young lads who helped in the sickbay of eighteenth century 'Men of War'. They took their name from the gruel that was served to the sick and injured and referred to as Loblolly. One small lane within the grounds of Haslar will soon bear the name Loblolly Lane.*

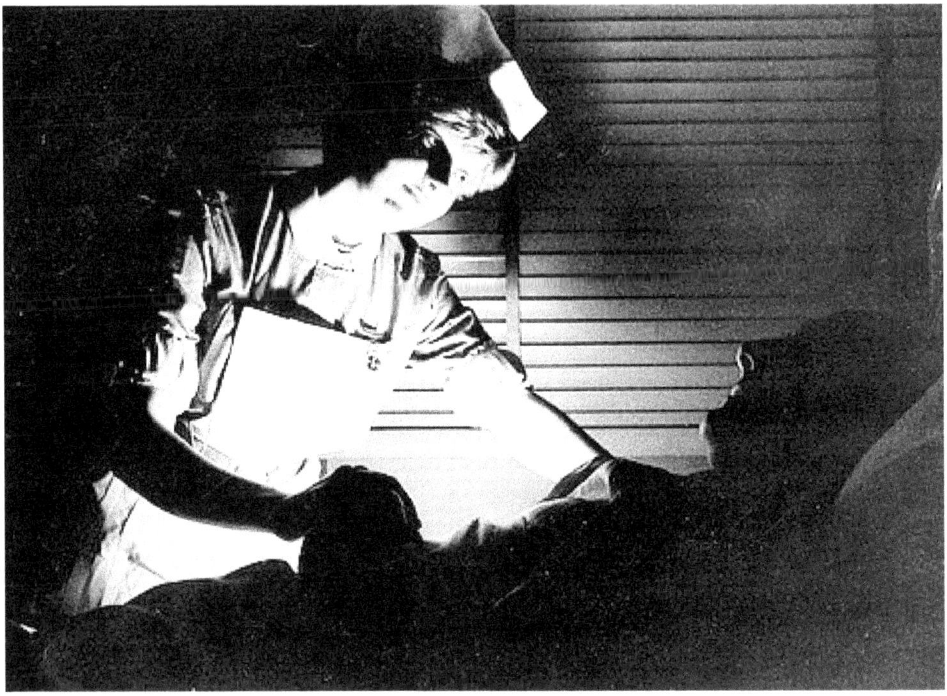

Night Nurse: an evocative recruiting picture of patient care on the night watch

Don't forget my Guinness!

I was in the Royal Navy from 1964 to 1985 and around 1973 I was admitted to Haslar as a patient, when I had a chronic disc problem in my lower back.

They initially put me on traction, which seemed worse than the original problem, but the discomfort was relieved every evening, not by the Drugs Round but by the Drinks Trolley*. Each day we were given an issue of beer etc – in my case, a can of Guinness. On the day of my operation, I got the guy in the next bed to promise that he would get my Guinness so I could enjoy it when I came round from the anaesthetic.

Imagine the scene later when I was only half awake as the drinks trolley arrived but – safe in the knowledge that my new 'Oppo' would do the right thing – I relaxed. However, he got chatting to the nurse and forgot my order. It was all I could muster but I managed to get her attention as the trolley whisked past my pit. I got my Guinness and promptly went back to sleep.

Bill Fewtrell

During the 1950s, 60s and early 70s Brickwood's Beer was delivered to the hospital and each patient – as agreed by the Medical Officer – was given a bottle of beer each evening. Officers were permitted spirits and sometimes the rules were bent or even broken.

Three in a row

In the 1970s the staff at Haslar were still mainly military but they allowed civilians to be admitted. I had three visits to Haslar.

The first came after a call from a staff nurse at the Emergency room: my husband Andrew, who was night fishing on his boat off of the Needles, had been rescued by the lifeboat after the coastguard had spotted flames. The nurse said Andrew was suffering from burns and exposure; thankfully Haslar was close by and their expertise was on hand immediately. He was soon released home after fast and expert treatment.

The second call came from my dad, who had been working with my husband on a demolition site in Gosport. He said Andrew had snapped off a window latch but had slipped, slashing his wrist – again Haslar and their brilliant staff were close at hand and saved his life after he lost a great deal of blood.

The third was when my son, aged 10 months, started convulsing; I was young and naive and knew nothing of convulsions. We were terrified. The ambulance had to come from Fareham owing to a busy night, the new Haslar bridge had only opened that day and they were unsure of the way, but I was so glad to arrive at Haslar and to be swept into the care of the paediatric staff. They took immediate care of our baby and gave us huge support. Hospitals at that time did not like parents to stay outside of visiting hours but I was welcomed and given a bed alongside his cot. I could not praise the staff highly enough for their care.

Radiance McLaren-Draper

Gallows humour

For many years Haslar received patients involved in civilian motoring (me included) or other serious accidents. It was quite common to hear the expression 'Thank God we have Haslar on our doorstep' when referring to such incidents.

My recollections of Haslar consist of an overnight stay in the 1960s surrounded by Naval patients who had gallows humour. A seaman in the bed next to mine asked why I had been admitted and I told him it was for overnight observation following a motorcycle accident when my head hit the road.

"Oh," he replied, "my shipmate had that happen and he looked perfectly fine but died two days later!"

On the morning of my release a passing doctor said the doctor's round (to sign me off) wouldn't be for another two hours, so why didn't I pop over to the NAAFI canteen and have a pint?

Colin Young

A little experiment

When I was 15, I fell off a high wall at the rear of Richmond Road, Gosport, where I was living, and broke my left arm.

I went to the War Memorial Hospital and was transferred to Haslar. Because my arm was broken right up to the ball socket, my parents were informed I would have to stay in hospital for treatment.

I was put on the orthopaedic ward and was the only civilian and youngster on a ward of about 20 men. At this time, only Navy personnel ran the hospital and the other men on the ward were all in the Navy.

Because of my injury, Surgeon Commander Pugh said he was going to try an experiment on me, as it would be very awkward to plaster my complete shoulder and arm. My arm was held in a raised position for two days to allow the bone to drop down and then they pushed it up for it to knit together. I made a full recovery and I used to sometimes attend seminars at which Surgeon Commander Pugh was giving a talk. At these Seminars, he showed my X-rays to the audience and I stood at the front where he demonstrated the full movement that I had regained with the treatment he had given me.

Ironically, I ended up working at Haslar for the Department of the Environment as a Maintenance Fitter for 12 years, before leaving to join the Fire Service.

Eddie Taylor

Not yet, son!

I was a receptionist in the radiology department and one day my daughter-in-law brought in my grandson, who was five at the time.

A porter was bringing down a patient on a bed. My grandson looked at her lying there and said loudly:

"I think that lady's dead."

We were so embarrassed, but the lady just laughed and said:

"Not yet, son."

Margaret Cowell

It had to be a Naval surgeon

My memories go back to the late 1950s. My step-grandfather, Commodore Allan Peachey CBE DSO, required an operation to straighten his fourth finger. Although a member of BUPA since its inception and a London resident, he would not trust anyone but a naval surgeon for the delicate surgery.

I remember the whole family driving him to Haslar, but I was not permitted to visit being too young (probably under 10 years of age). The operation was very successful even though he suffered a frozen shoulder during his recuperation. A difficult man to please, he was delighted with the outcome and would be very sad to know of the demise of this great hospital.

Louise Paterson

Tiny Tears in trouble

I was eight years old when I went into Haslar to have my tonsils out in 1972 and remember taking my Tiny Tears dolly with me for comfort. I got told off by a nurse because I fed my dolly some of my Ribena and she wet the bed with a Ribena stain all over the white starched sheets. I don't think I was very popular, but the memory has always stayed with me.

Trudie Doughty

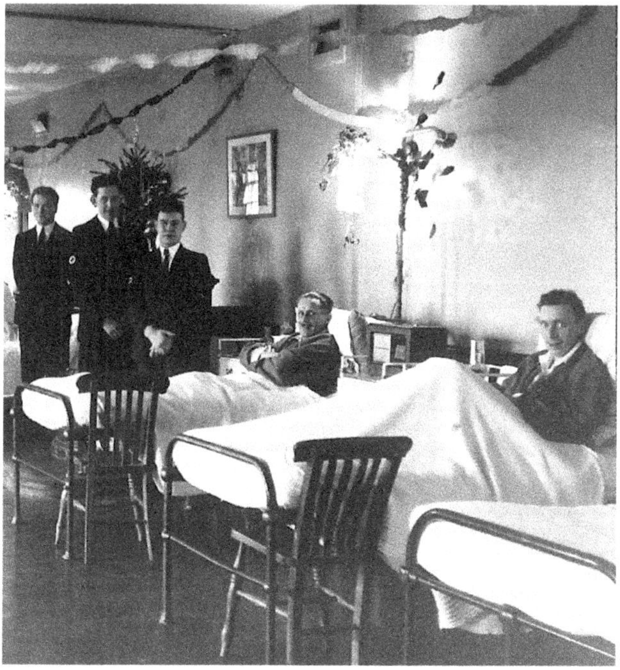

Sick Berth ward staff with patients at Christmas

All that – and six children too!

As a psoriasis sufferer, I first attended Haslar as an outpatient back in the 1970s and remained as an outpatient until I moved to Bristol with my job in 1996. Commander Richard Ashton was my Consultant and was well respected in the field of dermatology. I had the utmost confidence and respect in him even when my condition on a few occasions became severe, requiring my admittance for treatment as an inpatient.

There was one particular incidence back in the late 80s when I was recovering at home after a sinus operation at Haslar and my psoriasis started to flare up. The flare-up continued over a number of days and coincided with severe sinus pain. I phoned the Dermatology Department and Dr Ashton agreed to see me that morning.

Following a review of my skin, he confirmed that I needed to be admitted but was also concerned that my sinuses might be infected, so left me in his consulting room to find his ENT (Ear Nose and Throat) colleague who had an outpatient clinic close by. They returned a few minutes later, confirmed that I had a severe infection, and jointly agreed – to my astonishment – that I should be admitted to a ward that day for a course of treatment for my psoriasis and sinus infection.

Dr Ashton's propensity for work was well known and as well as his naval and civilian Skin Clinics and running a private clinic at weekends, he also attended numerous conferences and wrote a number of books on dermatological conditions and treatments. This in itself was astonishing but the most amazing thing was that he had six children (although this number may have increased after I moved to Bristol!).

Simon Pearce

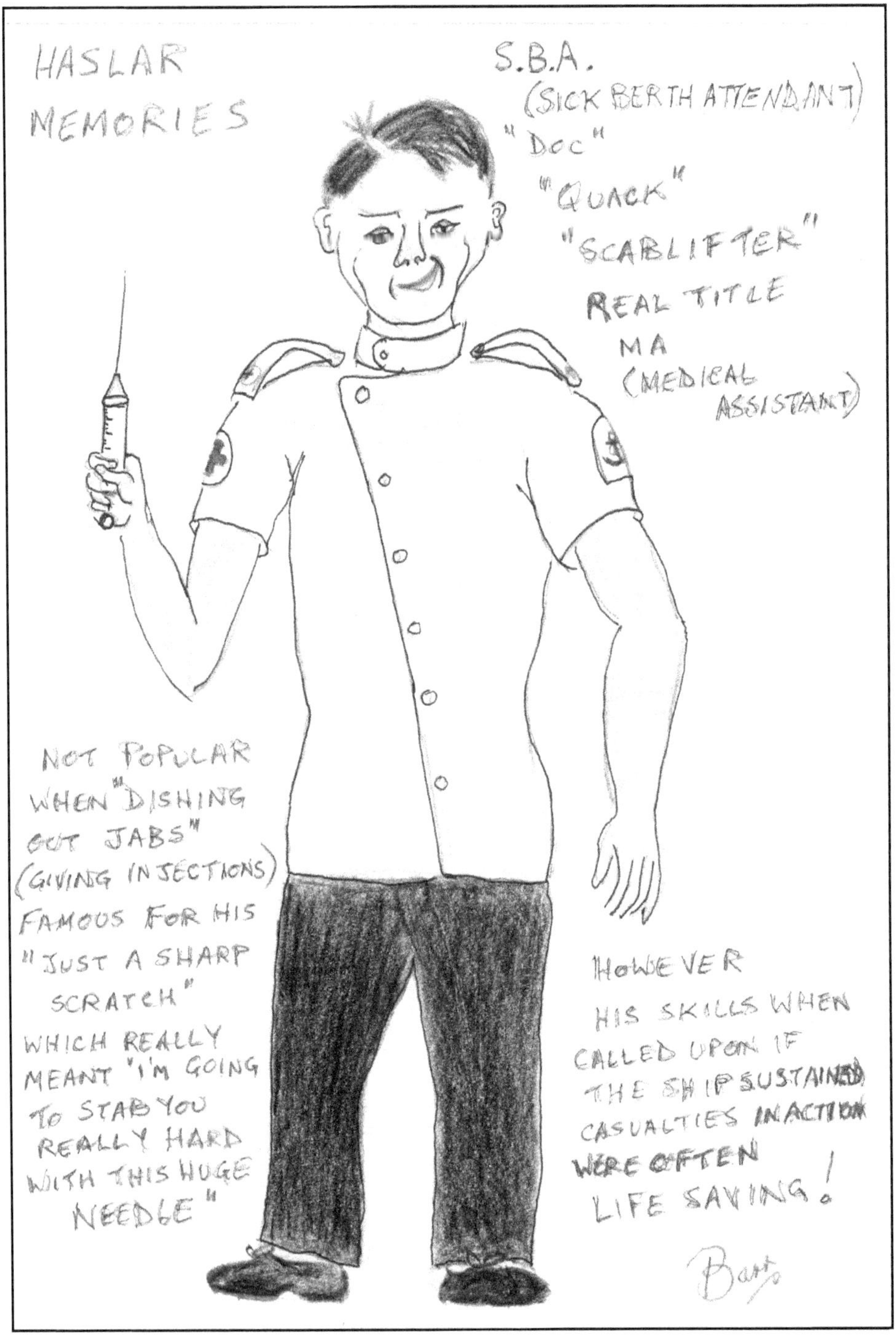
HASLAR MEMORIES
S.B.A. (SICK BERTH ATTENDANT)
"DOC"
"QUACK"
"SCABLIFTER"
REAL TITLE MA (MEDICAL ASSISTANT)
NOT POPULAR WHEN "DISHING OUT JABS" (GIVING INJECTIONS) FAMOUS FOR HIS "JUST A SHARP SCRATCH" WHICH REALLY MEANT "I'M GOING TO STAB YOU REALLY HARD WITH THIS HUGE NEEDLE"
HOWEVER HIS SKILLS WHEN CALLED UPON IF THE SHIP SUSTAINED CASUALTIES IN ACTION WERE OFTEN LIFE SAVING!
Bart

QARNNS
QUEEN ALEXANDRA'S ROYAL NAVAL NURSING SERVICE
HASLAR MEMORIES
ANSWERING THE CRY "CAN I HAVE A BOTTLE PLEASE NURSE" WAS ONE OF THEIR LESS PLEASANT THEIR DUTIES - BUT THEIR WHITE STARCHED UNIFORMS (AND BLACK STOCKINGS!) WOULD PUT A SMILE ON THE FACE OF ANYONE UNLUCKY ENOUGH TO BE CONFINED TO SICK BAY, WHATEVER THEIR MALADY!
THEIR WORK ON BOARD HOSPITAL SHIPS IN TIMES OF CONFLICT IS THE STUFF OF LEGEND!

An adult education

In 1974/5, when I was a young schoolboy, I had a bad sporting accident and ended up at Haslar for treatment. It was then a pioneering serious operation performed by a Surgeon Commander. It was very unusual for a civilian, never mind a young child, to be treated in the Naval Hospital.

I was on a ward of about 30 others, all sailors, all much older than me and spent the weeks there being taught how to play cribbage.

I remember a middle-aged sailor who woke from his anaesthetic early, sat up in bed, pointed at me and shouted: "Get that f****ng parrot off that tree!' before falling back immediately to his slumber.

The operation I had was later performed on Prince Charles and described as a 'first' – but the surgeons at Haslar had done that long before!

Steve Sykes

Eternal thanks

I have two reasons to be thankful and grateful for having trained at Haslar. I joined up in October 1977, as a pupil nurse as part of F class and met 12 wonderful girls, most of whom I would spend the next two years with while we honed our skills and learned how to be the best nurses in the country. My training and the standards I learned have stayed with me my whole life.

However, despite being a proud ex-QARNN I have another reason for being grateful to Haslar and its staff because they saved my life in 1987 after an accident. I was badly injured and arrived at theatre haemorrhaging, with barely a pulse. Three operating staff Medical Assistants was the only ones there to meet me. Shocked that their patient was one of their colleagues, and horrified at my condition, they kept their heads, remembered their training and kept me alive until anaesthetists and surgeons arrived. They then assisted with the surgery during the next 10 hours, saving my life and my right leg. Then my colleagues in Intensive Care found their friend was there as a patient rather than working alongside them. Many people – nurses, doctors, physios, family and friends – got me through those tough months.

Ultimately I had to leave the service that I loved. However, I have never let that accident define me, even though I have lived with the after-affects ever since that tragic day. I truly believe my training and the things I had learned helped me cope with what happened.

Even now, years later, I am still learning new things about that night and I am grateful for the messages and things I have been told. I know I am so lucky to have survived and still be here living life to the full.

So my eternal thanks and gratitude go to Haslar and its staff, for making me the proud nurse I still am today and for saving my life so I could continue in the profession I love.

Lorraine Scaife

Jealous of the uniforms

I'm writing this from Queensland Australia where I now live.

I was a patient with Haslar in 1984. I was playing tennis and completely ruptured my achilles tendon. The care and attention I got was excellent. My sister-in-law was a nurse at the time in Northamptonshire. I remember her being very jealous of the lovely uniforms when she came to visit me at Haslar.

My tendon was successfully repaired by surgery and intense physiotherapy at the hospital. I completed two London marathons along with many other races and continued to play tennis. I'm now 65, and to this day have never had a single problem with it. The very long scar is barely visible, so thank you so much for the care and attention I received.

Gill Sickling

My first and last cigarette

The year was 1976 and I was 16 years old. I was injured at HMS *Raleigh* on an assault course and as my home town was Portsmouth the Navy moved me from RNH Stonehouse hospital to Haslar.

My first experience was collecting the beer ration for a party at the weekend. Each day we were issued with a can of beer or a tot of rum; the older men in the ward told me to stockpile the beer until the weekend.

The weekend came and the nurse – who was a Wren – got me out of bed, placed me in a wheelchair and took me for a breath of air outside ... only to be taken into the hospital grounds where the older gents were having a party. I drank the beer and smoked my first and last cigarette, coughing my lungs out as I did it.

The other memory was being asked if I wanted a hot, or cold bedpan, only to find out this was a trick question. It either came straight out of the steam sterilisation machine or the icebox – this was offered to all new young patients.

Mum always said I entered the Navy a boy and left a man: if only she knew what made me grow up!

Alan Prior

A bath full of Mackeson

I joined the Royal Navy in March 1953 at the age of 16, signed up for 12 years then contracted tuberculosis (TB) and entered Haslar in October of that year. I spent six months undergoing treatment and was invalided out of the Navy in April 1954. So much for a career at sea!

However, my time in Haslar was very enlightening for an innocent 17-year-old boy. I recall that along with the daily injections we were issued with a bottle of Mackeson's Milk Stout, which we carefully stowed away in one of the bath tubs for Christmas (the bath was full by Christmas Day – lovely!)

Christmas Day on the ward for Zymotics: Tony is pictured third from left holding his new pint glass

As it was a TB ward there was a verandah for 'fresh air' treatment and I remember my Oppo and I pushing our beds out on to the verandah and spending a couple of nights out there playing the children's game 'Battleships' with paper and pencils. This was also the time of the 1953 Coronation Fleet Review and we had a good view of the various ships at anchor.

Other recollections are having the beds made (envelope corners!) and sitting to attention for Medical Officer's 'rounds'.

Tony Thatcher

Sweeney and the ice-cream

I was in Haslar Hospital when I was five to have my tonsils removed: it was 1966 and England won the World Cup while I was there. In the bed next to me was a sailor called Sweeney – I guess that was because his surname was Todd. He looked after me when I was in recovery and made sure I had plenty of ice-cream.

My second visit to Haslar was in 1974 when I was 13. On Bonfire Night, I got hit by a large plank of wood and was knocked out – I had a huge lump on my head.

I also worked in Haslar as a Groundsman for a year in 1977, cutting the grass and keeping the grounds tidy. My favourite job was the cutting the grass on the tennis courts and marking out the white lines. The courts where right in front of the nurses' block and I was often caught watching them sunbathe and duly reprimanded.

Haslar was a big part of my life. My mum, dad, wife and children have all been treated there: it was a truly wonderful hospital

Terry Archer

CHRISTMAS DAY
1953

ROYAL NAVAL
HOSPITAL HASLAR

MENU

BREAKFAST

BACON, EGG & SAUSAGE
ROLLS & BUTTER
MARMALADE
COFFEE

DINNER

CREAM OF TOMATO SOUP
ROAST TURKEY
SAUSAGE STUFFING
ROAST POTATOES
SPROUTS & FRESH PEAS
CHRISTMAS PUDDING
RUM SAUCE
FRUIT & NUTS

TEA

TEA, BREAD & BUTTER
JAM
CAKE, BISCUITS
JELLIES, TRIFLE

SUPPER

OXTAIL SOUP
COLD HAM
COLD ROAST PORK
PICKLES
MINCE PIES

HASLAR

A calorie-packed day: the Christmas Day menu from 1953

An evil look on her face

I moved into the area in 2006 from South London having already had a left hip replacement the previous year, but because of a few complications I had to have a revision. Haslar Hospital was where it was to be done.

On Sunday 18 June 2007 I was admitted to the mixed ward (men one end of the ward, women the other). Straight away the ward Sister mildly reprimanded me for not bringing my blood pressure tablets, but in a jovial kind of way. The next day was the day of the operation and when I came out of the anaesthetic I vaguely remember nurses and doctors scurrying around me with some concern: apparently I'd had low blood pressure, a fact with which I ribbed the Sister.

The following day I got myself out of my bed and sat in a chair next to it reading (I hate lying in bed) when in walked Dr Langdon, the surgeon who had carried out the operation. He was quite amazed that I was out of bed chatting to other patients and nurses in between chapters of my book (Pele's biography). After he had proudly displayed the old prosthesis that he'd removed from my hip he used my mobile phone to take a photograph of it, which I still have to this day. He then went across to the nurse in charge and I heard him refer to me as being phenomenal.

The one incident that will be etched on my memory for as long as live was when the Sister came to remove my catheter. As she pulled the curtains round she looked at me with what seemed like an evil grin (remember, I'd been giving her a lot of cheeky banter). She then stood at the end of bed, not once taking her eyes off me, as she pulled on her surgical gloves, deliberately snapping them against her wrists as she did so. She then called out to the rest of the ward: "If you hear a scream, don't worry – it's only Mr Fry letting you know that I've taken out his catheter!" I should have known she'd get the last laugh, because I did laugh quite a bit while in there and that has to be a good tonic for any post-operative patient.

The next two days were spent in the capable hands of the physiotherapist. I was discharged on the following Thursday with some good memories of what I initially thought was an old-fashioned hospital, which would no doubt have old-fashioned methods. How wrong I was! Over the past twelve years I've had four major operations in four different hospitals involving joint replacements and although I've experienced professional care in all four hospitals, it's Haslar the
holds the best memories.

Dave Fry

Not exactly a soft landing

Way back in 1956, I was a young Naval Air Mechanic serving on board HMS *Bulwark* with 895 Squadron en route to Suez, to give naughty President Nasser a slap on the wrist. However on reaching Malta, the ship had to transfer supplies to HMS *Eagle* on the other side of Grand Harbour. This involved bringing the stores, which were in the form of large wooden crates, up from the hangar on the forward lift and loading them into a cargo net. This was then lifted by a floating crane and lowered into a lighter alongside. From there it was transported across to Eagle where the same operation took place in reverse.

The first load went off without incident, but the second load began to fall out of the cargo net as it was lifted by the crane. I was in the party on the flight deck underneath the falling crates, so obviously we all scattered in every direction! The lift had already gone down to collect the next load and unfortunately as I turned to escape the falling crates I stepped into the space where the lift should have been. A thirty-foot drop onto an armoured steel deck was not a soft landing! Multiple injuries were sustained. After two weeks in Bighi, the RN Hospital outside Valetta, it was decided to send home as many patients as possible to make way for any wounded from the forthcoming Suez hostilities. So I was flown back to the UK courtesy of RAF Transport Command in the form of a rickety old Hastings aircraft, which did nothing for my peace of mind as I was strapped in a stretcher with one arm, both legs, and my back encased in plaster of Paris! We landed safely at Lyneham, and after one night in RAF Wilton hospital were taken by road to Haslar.

As I was being carried in on a stretcher, I looked up at those ancient vaulted ceilings and grand Victorian architecture and fully expected Florence Nightingale to appear. In fact it was a wonderful Queen Alexandra Royal Nursing Service sister in her magnificent starched white headdress.

Recuperation was rapid once in Haslar, due in the most part to some amazing physiotherapy that took the form of hanging me from the wall bars in the gym with threats of physical violence if I dared to let go/ Tough love was what they called it. You did not get the chance to feel sorry for yourself and it certainly worked wonders for me, because ten weeks after my accident I went home on leave.

Some months later when the ship returned to Pompey I went back on board – to the surprise of many who assumed I had been killed!

Barry Prosser

I've got the scar to remind me

Back in 1997 I became quite unwell with an excruciating pain in my hip area. My GP at the time thought it was a kidney infection so gave me an injection and a pill for the pain. A week later, I started to get the pain again and was admitted to Haslar where I passed a kidney stone. After I was released, I was told it was uncommon for a thirty-three year old to pass a kidney stone, so I had to have scans to determine if I had a tumour on one or more of my parathyroid glands, which of course turned out to be the case. I went back into Haslar where I had a five-hour operation to remove the tumour. I still have the scar on my neck and it reminds me of Haslar and how wonderful the nurses, doctors and of course the surgeons were.

Catherine Wilson

A bionic arm

I was a patient at Haslar after breaking my right elbow on falling off an Exmoor pony on my first bareback ride across Gilkicker. The break smashed my elbow very badly – I think I must have landed on a brick and I believe at one point they thought my arm might have to be amputated. I was 13 years old.

Luckily for me, Lieutenant Commander Philip Fulford was just off the Royal Yacht and was able to perform two operations that had not been done before – and with no metal inserted! Then, after six months of swimming physiotherapy in their small pool, I had a bionic arm that was brilliant with just a neat four-inch scar.

To this day I am so very grateful to that tall, handsome gentleman and to Haslar.

Louise Reece

Give us a kiss, Matron

My father Sid Leyland (former Councillor, Deputy Mayor and Mayor of Gosport) was in hospital at Haslar twice. He liked the fact that patients were allowed to make themselves cups of tea and cocoa in the evenings and that the atmosphere in the wards was very informal.

On his second stay he was visited by the Captain of Haslar, who asked him if there was anything he could do to help. Dad said that he was upset at having to miss the Rugby League Challenge Cup Final on the Saturday coming. The Captain said he was sure that something could be arranged. At 2pm a sailor arrived at his bedside with a wheelchair and took him to the Captain's office, where the sailor and dad watched the game on a very large colour television.

When I was living in Liverpool, I met an old man who had been a patient at Haslar during the First World War. Jim Sidwell told me that discipline was very strict. One day a senior officer did a tour of inspection. Due to an earlier incident, Jim was punished by having to remain in bed for the rest of the day. When the officer asked why the man was in bed and not sitting by his bed like the other men on the ward, he was told that it was for disciplinary reasons. The officer asked Jim what he had done and he explained that he had asked the Matron for a kiss. The officer nodded and went away.

The following day Jim was asked to be dressed and at the main entrance at 2pm. A car and chauffeur arrived to take him on a drive round the Hampshire countryside and then to a house on a large estate for tea. He had a big tea in the servants' kitchen and was given cakes to take back to the hospital for the other men on the ward.

The chauffeur explained that he thought that asking the matron for a kiss was the action of a very brave man.

Maxine Leyland

Its 17:00, gentlemen

During my long service career I became a patient of Haslar four times.

The February weather of 1950 was atrocious and like many others I suffered heavy colds, which in my case rapidly became flu then bronchitis. I was taken by ambulance from Royal Naval Barracks (Nelson) to Haslar and was carried into one of those wards overlooking the sea.

The ward was very basic with a large Dickensian fire in the centre – fine if you were near to it – and it was full of coal. My condition fluctuated from hot to cold, and I was shaking and weak. Despite my situation I staggered to the toilet overlooking the sea at the end of the ward. I couldn't face the alternative. What a sight! The floor was swamped and the old sash windows rattled as the sea and gale-force winds crashed against them. At this point I passed out and came alive in my bed, receiving well-deserved chastisement from Matron.

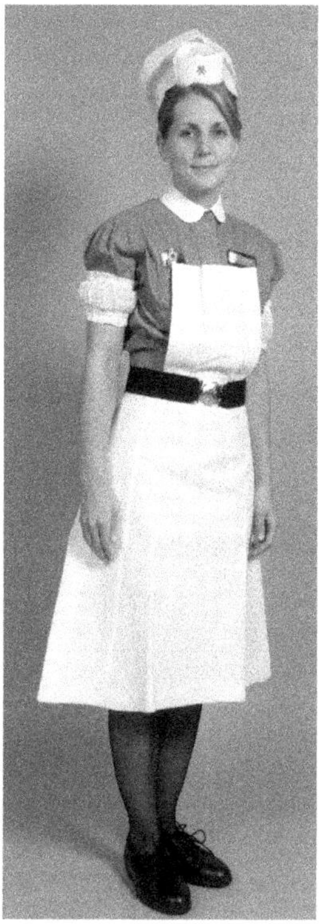 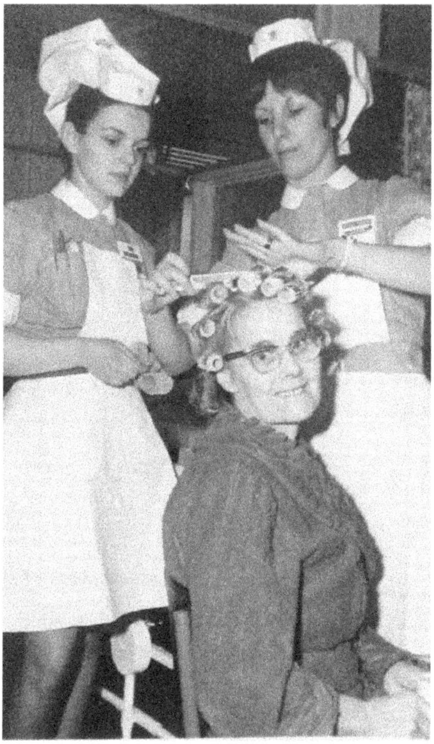 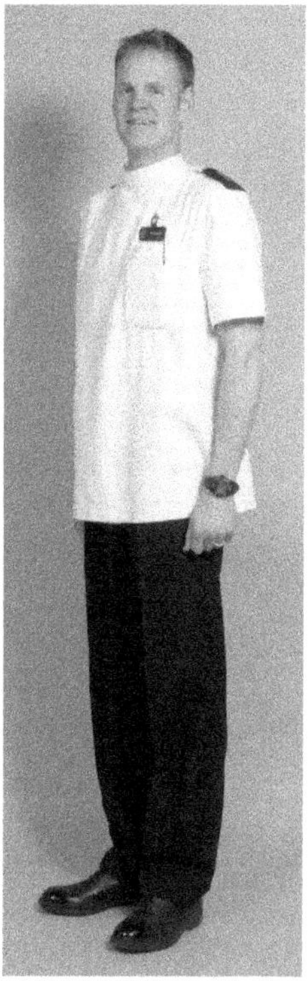

Centre: Hair-care on the ward for long-term patients. Left: A QARNNS SRN Nurse. Right: A Royal Navy Medical Assistant

After some time I was pronounced fit and returned to duty. This time I boarded the Haslar hospital launch, with its Red Cross and large hatches to take the stretcher cases.

My next visit, still in the 1950s, was for an ingrowing toe nail and lasted TWO WEEKS. This did allow for a reserve of 'walking wounded', able to fetch coal and haul the long-handled floor polishers known as bumpers – the timber floors were always very shiny.

We all loved the nurses, impeccable in their highly starched uniforms, always cheerful and helpful – nothing ever seemed too much trouble for them.

Some years later I was admitted for an operation on my bunions: both big toes were to be broken and reset. Surgeon Captain Jones was the senior orthopaedic and was affectionately known as 'Jones the Bones', bless him.

I was now promoted and joined the well-known officers' ward (A3 I think) where we were thoroughly spoilt, just a small ward of 16 or so. We had a lot of fun: at 1700 hours every evening one of us would announce "its 1700, gentlemen" whereupon all would open their lockers and produce gin, tonic, brandy etc. It was cocktail party time. It was fun both for patients and staff in A3.

After the operation both feet were plastered up to my knees then covered by large canvas walking boots. I was then returned to my duties on the waterfront of HMS *Vernon* (now Gunwharf Quays) amid peals of laughter.

Several years on I returned to Haslar for my fourth visit, this time to treat my varicose veins. While bedridden on this occasion I mentioned my failing eyesight – so I was wheeled down to the eye department for testing. Such extra treatment was commonplace; we were so well cared for at Haslar.

Doug Barlow

Even the cleaners were chatty

I was a patient at Haslar in September 1990 to have my gall bladder removed. Commander Leicester was my surgeon. I stayed in for four days and was treated very kindly by all the male and female nurses. Even the cleaners were chatty and lovely. It was a fantastic tri-Service hospital and wonderful staff.

Lorraine Gee

No sugar-coating

My father was urgently sent for tests when he became ill in 1993. He was diagnosed with bowel cancer and referred to a very nice consultant, Commander Dale. This Commander had a very abrupt way of explaining things to you, but in hindsight it was just his manner and he wasn't one to sugar-coat anything!

He was particularly interested in dad, as this was a hereditary disease. We were told that Commander Dale really was the best in his field of work and this proved correct: after a few scary operations, dad was out of the woods. The Commander kept the whole of the intestine that he'd removed for his students, as he said it was interesting, and on the other hand it was the worst he had seen! Using a new technique, he reconstructed a new 'bowel'. QA consultants are baffled by this even now. Some 24 years on, we have a lot to thank Commander Dale for.

Kerry Webster

A nine o'clock appointment

I broke my leg in an accident at work in September 1981 and was airlifted to Haslar by HMS *Daedalus* Search and Rescue. I was then taken to A&E where I was treated, given pain relief, put in a temporary plaster and discharged.

I then returned to Haslar fracture clinic on the Monday with a nine o'clock appointment, and on arrival it seemed that everyone had nine o'clock appointments. After having an X-ray, I waited to see the Consultant, who was a Naval Officer. When he saw me he became quite animated and was shouting at some staff about why I was sent home and not admitted when I had first arrived. I got the impression that someone was in trouble. He wanted me admitted straight away and he could not apologise enough. I was admitted to a ward and then operated on the following day. I was placed in a full cast – hip to ankle. I was given excellent treatment from then on and the staff were fantastic. I was allowed home after seven days with follow-up appointments made for the fracture at … yes, you`ve guessed it … nine o'clock.

After four weeks at home and being nearly immobile because of the weight and size of the plaster, I contracted pneumonia and was returned to Haslar for another seven days. The care and attention was second to none and the once again the staff were fantastic, always having a laugh and making patients comfortable: nothing was too much trouble for them. I had trouble initially sleeping at night and I remember playing chess and Scrabble with the night nurses.

Overall my experience at Haslar was one of being made to feel valued and not a burden.

Mark Davis

Open wide!

I was serving in HMS *Dainty* based in Portsmouth during the mid-1960s. The Medical Officer on board sent me to see the dentist at Haslar as I was having trouble with my teeth. When I arrived at his surgery he took one look at them and said: "Two wisdom teeth have to come out"

The Sick Berth Attendant, who was the dental assistant, held me to the chair with an arm around my neck and the dentist – bracing himself on my chest with his knee – proceeded to pull them out one by one before the pain-dulling jab had taken effect. I fainted and the next thing I knew I was upside down with my head to the floor, still strapped in the chair. When they saw I had come around again they upended me, told me to swill my mouth out and sent me on my merry way back to my ship. I haven't been a fan of dentists since.

Alan Petrie

Urban Farm animals came to Haslar

My memories relate to me and my family, plus volunteers, attending the yearly fetes that Haslar held. We provided an animal 'hands-on experience', taking along a variety of stock from our Community Urban Farm at Hardway known as Felicia Park. We set up a gazebo with enclosures for our ducks (along with their own pond), chickens, rabbits, guinea pigs, our two larger dogs, a couple of friendly cats and of course our miniature ponies. Some children had never been so close as to be able to handle and groom animals, so they really enjoyed it. We gave talks on their care and feeding, and sold goods to help with the funding for the farm.

I also attended Haslar as a patient following various accidents at the farm, twice being knocked over by horses going into their stables, having stitches in a sliced thumb, a nail taken from my foot and stitches to my ankle through broken glass. I always found the staff very helpful and friendly.

I watched the TV programme of 'Time Team' which showed the burial places of people from Nelson's time and determined their deaths and injuries using today's technology. If the walls of Haslar could talk, what fascinating stories they could tell! At one of the sales I now attend for funding for the wildlife I feed, I met a man who now lives in the Admirals's house. I asked him about ghosts, to which he replied there were some in the house and many in the hospital itself.

My brother, Brian Furlong, worked at Haslar for some years as an electrician and you can read his memories elsewhere in this book. Unfortunately he passed away shortly after submitting his memories.

I expect other readers will remember Brian as a workmate, or seeing him in their wards when they were patients there. I remember one story he told me of when my sister June Limber was in there. He wanted to visit her in his working hours, so decided to walk through the ward she was in, carrying a long ladder and pretending he was seeing to the lights. I think he gave it away by stopping to eat her grapes!

Sue Hitchman

Male nurse was called Taffy

I was taken to Haslar in 1981 when I was 11 years old. I'd broken my arm on the climbing frame at the Inn by the Sea, Lee On Solent. The staff at Haslar were amazing and very kind: I didn't have to wait in A&E very long. It was the first time I had met a male nurse. He told me his name was Taffy – I think that was a nickname for Welsh people back then. It was a beautiful building; all of my family received treatment there at some point.

Andrew Cousins

Radio Haslar lives on

I first became a patient at Haslar in November 1976 following a motorbike accident. Over the following years had five operations, almost entirely on C6 ward. I remember the care and thought that went in to rehabilitation. I was in hospital for two weeks, mandatory following any leg operation, followed by sick leave and then physiotherapy. Strange that we now know that cartilages can heal but in the 70s, out they came!

The occupational health trolley would come round and everyone made what models they could in the time spent on the ward. If you were mobile, you were on tea-making duty. If it was summer and the weather was good, the nursing staff would happily take you downstairs in the lift and set you out on the grass, bed, drips, vacuums and all.

I was returned to almost normal fitness by 1980. During the course of one of my physiotherapy classes in that wonderful department that brought only pain, I found one day after leg-raising classes that I couldn't get off the floor. They brought my surgeon downstairs, Commander Bob Telfer, who with the aid of X-rays found I had broken my back across but that it had re-healed … so they had to manipulate it under anaesthetic, or in layman's terms, re-break it.

Over the years, they did that three times until they could do it no more and an operation called a Hartley fusion was called for. I had that in 1994. This time the surgeon was the famed Mike Farquharson Roberts. At follow-up appointments I was introduced to Magnus McLaren, who looked after my spine until I left the Navy in 1997. I had a couple of nose jobs too, not to mention the numerous visits to A&E for stitches following rugby matches for Dolphin or for Gosport & Fareham rugby teams.

After I gave up sport, the arthritis settled in and the leg became a graunch, so in 2006 my left knee was replaced – and the right need in 2010, by none other than Magnus

McLaren. I see him about every two years for a review on my spine and my knees – it's like we're old friends.

I'm back in the gym and at 60, enjoying life, disabled a little bit and unable to walk far now, but healthy. Haslar looked after me.

In repayment, I joined the Hospital Radio Station in 1997 and have presented a programme every week since. Sadly Haslar shut, but Radio Haslar continued, even though it was now broadcasting to the War Memorial Hospital. I have enjoyed being the Chair of Radio Haslar for the last five years.

It is our 25th anniversary in March 2018 and we will rename the station Gosport's Hospital Radio Station, though we will keep our Royal Haslar logo and as much as we can of Radio Haslar. It's the blood of that hospital that gave us the life we have.

Paul Dodd

They treated me like a king

I did my National Service as a cook in the RAF in 1956 and while working in the kitchen, got a very poisonous foot. Unbeknown to me, the stud in the boot I was wearing had been pushing into my foot.

I went on leave but was in a lot of pain with my foot and couldn't even put it on the ground. My mother called the Navy doctor out and I was taken by ambulance to HMS *Collingwood* who sent me directly to Haslar. I was a patient there for ten weeks. All the time I was there they treated me like a king. I was the only RAF person in there at the time, and I was eighteen years old. I have only very fond and happy memories of the long stay I had at Haslar.

Nick Martin

RAF man Nick Martin

A pioneering operation

It was the summer of 1966 when, following a traffic accident, I was taken to Haslar with a broken arm and leg. Commander Pugh was the senior surgeon, but it was Lt Commander Hesketh who operated on me. He was a confident, slim, dark-haired man who always had his collar turned up. He performed what he said was the hospital's first 'AO' plating on my right femur, rather than the tried-and-tested pin down the middle of the bone – he also plated my left forearm.

The next morning he, together with several onlookers that included a physio, was at my bedside expecting me to be able to walk. Unfortunately my muscles were too bruised and it was another two days before I was on my feet. The worst thing about my accident was having to go back to Haslar one year later to have the plates removed from both my arm and leg.

I can't thank the hospital and nurses enough for looking after me – even though I was not service personnel. Many of the other patients in the large dormitory ward were seamen, including some sub-mariners who appeared to be of a different breed, with an interesting sense of humour.

Rick Pittard

To Haslar with TB

My granddad, Mr E Patterson, contracted tuberculosis while serving with the Navy. My gran is unsure of which ship he was on when taken to Haslar but is aware that he served on HMS *Belfast* among many others. He was about 26 years old when this happened. My granddad was born in Liverpool but lived his adult life in Glasgow when he wasn't serving in the Navy.

Laura Cranley

Outside the TB ward in 1952 or 1953: Laura's grandfather flanked by his wife (left) and her mother, visiting from Glasgow

Over the wall

This is a tale that Yvonne Birbeck (nee Richards) related to me often. Yvonne and Lesley Richards lived at 148/146 Clayhall Road to the rear of Haslar. As young children in the late 1950s and 60s they used to go to the Haslar sea wall and many a tuberculosis patient in Zymotics ward – the ward for infectious diseases – used to take the sea air on the balcony of the upper wards. They would throw envelopes with money for Yvonne and Lesley to go to Gina's shop in Clayhall and buy cigarettes for them. The girls would bring back the cigarettes and throw them in a package with the change back over the fence, earning themselves a few coppers at the same time.

Eric Birbeck

Full recoveries all round

I first encountered Haslar at the age of 17 when I was admitted to have my tonsils removed. Instead, I had a sinus operation, for which I was grateful, after hearing all the moaning and groaning of the other patients who had had this surgery.

Ten years later, when pregnant, I opted to go to Haslar for all my routine blood tests, as it was less traumatic than the War Memorial Hospital or the surgery. The wait was shorter and there was the added bonus of free car parking.

Five years later, my son was admitted for a week on traction having been diagnosed with Perthes Disease, a rare childhood condition that affects the hip. I can recall the intense feeling of guilt, leaving my five-year-old in hospital while I was at work, but every day after work I would visit, and he would be surrounded by lovely nurses playing with him and giving him toys. He was looked after extremely well and the treatment worked.

The next encounter with Haslar was when my first husband was transferred there from Southampton General, to recuperate from a brain haemorrhage. Again, he had superb care and went on to make a full recovery.

Many years later, my second husband woke up in the early hours with chest pains. At that time, we lived in Ashburton Road in Alverstoke village and within just six minutes of leaving home he was being treated by a small army of medics. The security man let me drive straight through to the ambulance station outside A&E. He was admitted for 48 hours but it turned out to be nothing serious.

I then broke my ankle and was treated at A&E with hardly any wait at all; plastered and sent home on crutches for six weeks.

The memory that will stay with me forever, however, is when my second husband and I attended Haslar for the results of a biopsy following tests at QA. It was 7 February 2001. We had an appointment to see Lieutenant Colonel Whiteoak (I will never ever forget him or his name!). We were last on the list and I just knew it would be bad news, but I was not prepared for the delivery of such bad news! Lieutenant Colonel Whiteoak was a huge man who was about to be deployed to the Middle East. He examined my husband and then said: "I am sorry, Mr Derry, but you have stomach cancer and there is nothing more I can do for you."

Fortunately, my husband had private medical insurance and so we asked for an immediate referral and all necessary tests were arranged there and then. I am pleased to say that he made a full recovery following chemotherapy and radical surgery.

Finally, my father had a knee operation in Haslar and I always remember the shiny clean floors, the smartly uniformed military medical staff and the beautiful gardens.

Lynne Derry

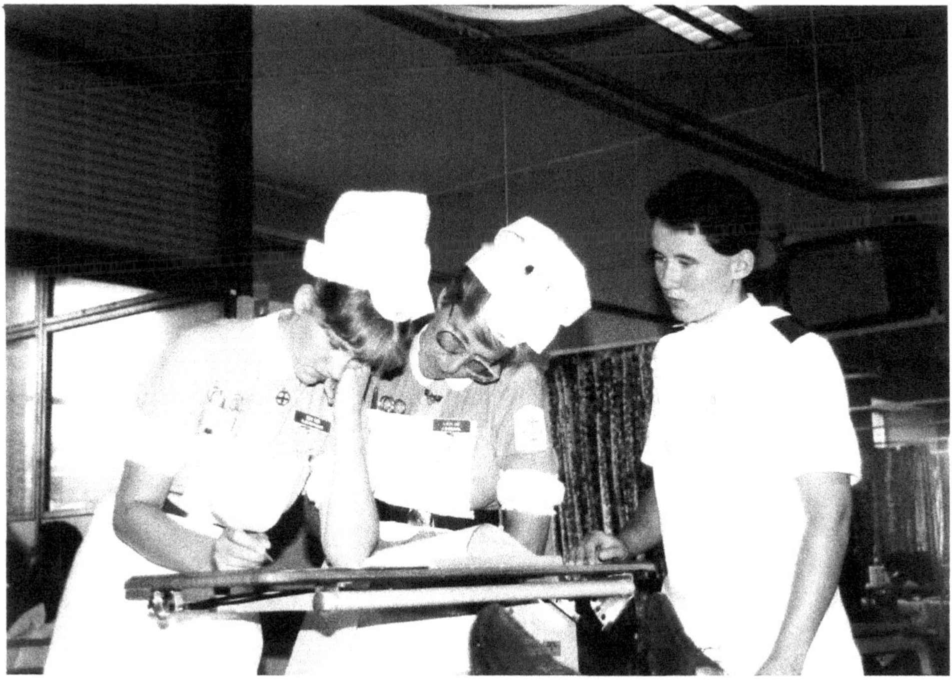

SEN Debbie Stephens, LNN Jo Gibbard and MA Justin James discuss a patient's record chart on F3 ward

Oh, it's you!

I was in Halar for a knee operation and was taken to theatre to have a pre-op check before being put to sleep. A Chief Medical Assistant walked in to take details. He was reading from documents and doing his checks. When he finished, he was almost out of the door when he turned to look at me. He took a step backwards in surprise. Once he had composed himself, he said: "What are you doing here? I didn't connect the patient name with you."

We knew each other through swimming: our paths had crossed perhaps at HMS *Temeraire*, the Navy's physical training establishment, or perhaps at a poolside somewhere in the country. It made a change for him to be in charge instead of me!

Hilary Essam

Like angels

My mum, Beryl Robins, was very religious and when she was in Haslar, the vicar was always there for her and spent many hours praying with her. She died in complete peace and comfort in October 2001 after being diagnosed with terminal cancer six months earlier. Her death was made easier for us as we knew she was not scared and she had been looked after so well. All of the nurses who cared for her were like angels for her.

Sarah Robins

Where's My Little Pony gone?

Between 1986 and 1991 I was a regular patient at Haslar children's ward. I suffered badly from atopic eczema and frequently needed inpatient treatment due to infections. Staff would bandage me from head to toe and I would even be sedated just to allow my skin to recover.

I have only fond memories of my times there. I remember arriving for one stay at about five years old and the quilt on the bed in my bay had a Transformers cover. The nurse turned and said: "Don't worry, Victoria, we still have the My Little Pony covers." I used to have a hard time sleeping, so as long as I was quiet I was allowed to sit and watch Postman Pat in my bay during the night.

One memory that sticks out very clearly was the playroom they had in the children's ward where there was a green plastic barrel. One evening I decided to crawl inside it then roll it out of the playroom down the ward. I was eventually stopped good naturedly by a nurse and asked to return it to the playroom before one of the sterner nurses discovered me. She tried (badly) not to laugh as I rolled my way back.

The staff was amazing and made my time away from home much less distressing at such a young age.

Victoria Stewart (née Laughton)

Close personal ties

My wife Linda and I have close family and personal associations with Haslar. Linda had skin cancer diagnosed there and I had three operations there, the first in 1976 when all the nursing staff were Royal Navy personnel. Linda's maternal grandfather, Randle Shenton, was an RN Ward Master around 1910 to 1918. My father, Walter Howard, worked there in the capacity of a civilian Steward on the Officers' Wards following retirement from the Royal Marines in 1946.

Derek Howard

Doing anything at Christmas?

My husband was diagnosed with bowel cancer in 1998 and was booked in at Haslar to see Commander Cripps, who asked us if we were doing anything at Christmas – so my husband had his first operation there. What a lovely reception we both had! My husband suffered from agoraphobia, which made things very difficult, but they made exceptions and I would go to the hospital at 10 in the morning and stay until 10 at night. The staff treated me wonderfully and made sure I had a dinner every day.

My husband unfortunately passed away in 2000, and so the story goes on. I was diagnosed with breast cancer at the end of that year and had three operations in Haslar. What a wonderful way they treated people! Although I have some sad memories of it, I can only sing my praises. And finally, what surgeon would send you a message of condolence after your husband had passed away? I still have the letter that he sent me. Commander Cripps at the time was serving on *Illustrious*.

Pamela Tree

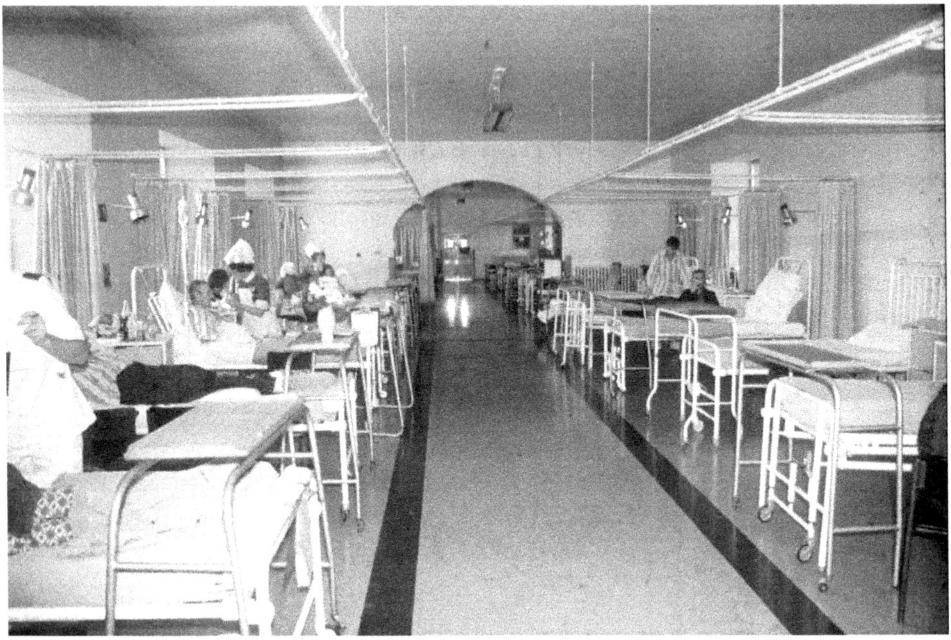

A ward in the 1970s or 1980s

Winston put me at ease

I had two knee replacements done at Haslar, one in 2007 the other in 2008, just before it closed in 2009. There were wonderful surgeons, nurses and other staff – one I remember, a man called Winston, really put me at ease.

My knees are still OK except for some aches around the muscles. It's nice to be able to get around better as I have rheumatoid arthritis, and am now 81 years old.

Rita Muston

First class every time

In the early 1970s, in his Navy days, my late dad was an in-patient at Haslar. He had a slipped disc in his back and was in a plaster vest for some time. It seemed a really excellent, pleasant hospital even then.

Much later on, in 2001, I was a patient there for a short time. I had a double hernia, and a routine operation to fix it. The RAF Surgeon explained the problem and the operation to me very clearly and professionally. All went perfectly well, and the service was first class.

Then in 2008, I was sent to Haslar Outpatients two or three times for EEG (brainwave) tests and check-ups, and to see a heart specialist, after I had suddenly collapsed a few times, and blacked out once. The Army Medics there were excellent, efficient and friendly.

My daughter was once treated there for a fractured ankle/lower leg after a fall. Once again, it was first class in the Casualty Outpatients, including the X-ray and plaster cast.

My partner and I joined the 'Save Haslar' marches, walking right down there the first time, then right along the High Street on several occasions. Gosport Councillor Peter Edgar and some other very knowledgeable people made some very good, positive speeches outside the Town Hall but our MP, Peter Viggers, was nowhere to be seen. I'd heard he was apparently on the original 'Save Haslar Taskforce' years before, but he seemed to do nothing whatsoever then about trying to save Haslar.

We saw some more of Haslar's lovely grounds and some buildings on a Heritage Open Day in September a few years ago. Unbeknown to us, there is a lovely, peaceful memorial garden somewhere around the back of the grounds.

I wonder if they'll ever create a Haslar Museum as a fitting memorial to the great place?

Tony Heath

Only a whisper

I was in Haslar in April 1970 having a thyroid operation, which did not go well. The man who did the operation managed to damage my vocal cords, which left me unable to speak, only to whisper. It was eight months before people could hear me. I used to be able to sing, but I still can't, all these years later.

I was opposite the Sister's office on day when she came out and called for a nurse. Four times she shouted for a nurse and no-one came. She then pressed the cardiac arrest button and three arrived. It was to give a suppository to a patient. Very loudly she said to one nurse: "you know which end to put that, don't you?"

Jacqueline Pearson

You've just got to see this!

My memory is from 1992 when I was diagnosed with thyroid cancer at the age of just 22. Commander Barker was my surgeon and was an amazing man; he was so kind and explained everything properly.

I was in Haslar lots of times during my treatment and found myself mostly on the mixed wards: I was always the youngest by miles. These were the days before special wards for young cancer patients and it was all a bit scary for me.

My times were made easier by the staff, who recognised how traumatised by everything I was and often came to talk to me. Two young doctors in particular used to make me laugh so much with their pranks. One time when I was feeling particularly low, they told me to come with them as they had to practise a procedure that they thought I would be interested to see. They had to practise putting tubes up each other's noses and down into their stomachs! I watched in equal measure of hysterics and repulsion as these two took it in turns to clumsily put the tubes in place, with tears of pain and laughter streaming from their eyes.

Sometimes they sneaked sweets or magazines into the ward for me. They'd come and tell me funny stories whenever they went past. Once they told me to pretend I couldn't speak English when a new student came to examine me.

They certainly made a very distressing time much brighter. To them and all the staff that made me well again, I salute you!

Nicola Maasdam

Give me the antidote!

I was at Haslar in 1982 when I was eight years old, after falling out of a tree in Stanley Park and badly breaking my elbow and wrist. After waiting seven hours and having an X-ray where they had to straighten my broken arm (without any painkillers), I was finally hauled into the operating theatre just after midnight.

Apparently I was asking for 'antidote'. I don't know where I got that from, but I just wanted the drugs to knock me out! My mum spent the night in a spare bed. I remember my window overlooked the big yellow cradle that was raising the *Mary Rose*. I was there for three nights and distinctly remember the smell of the cast, which was made from Plaster of Paris.

Mark Jackson

Best hospital ever

Haslar was the best hospital ever. I – and members of my family – had several operations there. I had to go to A&E with my kids, and my treatment when I had a stroke was superb. The entire hospital was immaculately clean and the entire staff well trained, friendly, happy and helpful people. We will never see its like again.

Frances Patter

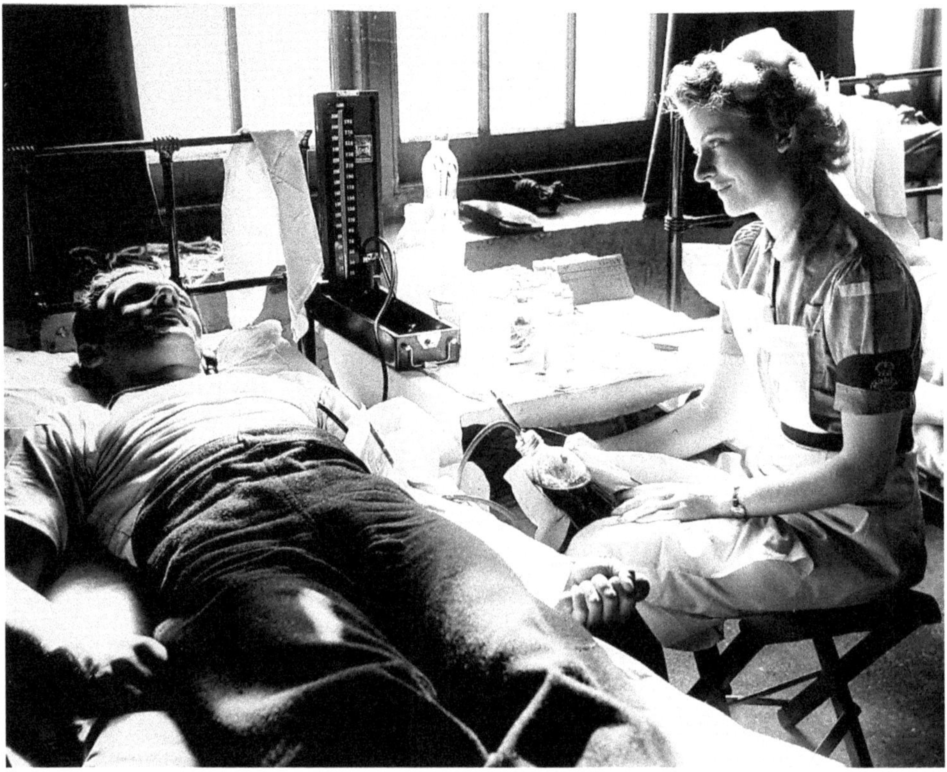

A VAD oversees the collection of blood as part of the Naval Blood Transfusion Service at Haslar during World War II

Glorious Technicolour

There came a time when Haslar was ordered to close down. Gosport knew it. Gosport hated it. But suddenly everyone in town seemed to find a chance for a medical lifeline. Whatever the future, it seemed everyone in town suddenly wanted answers to huge, sudden – real or imagined – pain.

My local dentist thought this was a great idea: "A chance to make sure there's nothing wrong I might have missed," he said. So there I was, on another trip to Haslar for a thorough examination of my teeth by a full Army colonel, no less.

"Do you put your teeth into a glass of water at night?" he asked. Long pause.

"What for?" I asked.

"Quite," he said. "There is no point in it. You know – they tell you these things in training – and of course you never really think about them."

Just when it looked like the last days for Haslar, there was an amazing number of men and women happy to have their intestines turned into a full-colour movie. The guy showed me the screen on the wall – "There's nothing wrong there, " he said. "But we might as well clear that bit …"

When I was fully awake, he handed me a tot of rum.

After a few years, even the most delicate of ladies would happily tell the story of their interior investigation … in colour, too.

John Bull

End of an era

One summer in France when we were on holiday at my parents' cottage, I fell over and badly sprained my ankle. We continued with our family holiday but I was aware that my ankle was becoming increasingly painful. Once back in Gosport, my friend Alyson insisted on driving me to the Haslar's A&E department to get my ankle checked out properly.

It was around 6 o'clock in the evening and, surprisingly, A&E was very quiet. The doctor on duty – who was a Captain in the Royal Navy – helped me into a wheelchair and remarked to the other staff that the X-ray machine was getting its very last patient!

I was indeed one of the final patients on that August evening, as, from 7 o'clock, all A&E cases were being referred elsewhere and the unit at Haslar was being closed for good.

As it turned out, I had broken my ankle, which was placed in a plaster cast.

The atmosphere was professional and the care exemplary. As the staff recalled their memories of the hospital, I felt that I had been privileged to witness the end of an era at a very special place.

As I left Haslar A&E and the doors closed behind me for the final time, it was a perfect and fitting gesture that the sunset was glorious: an image reflected in a hospital that had helped so many for so long.

Sally Hughes

Illustrious children

I mentioned to a friend about this up-coming book and she recounted a story of the Haslar visitors' book. It was on display so that the names of its illustrious visitors, including Admiral Lord Nelson, could be seen. Unfortunately this fact hadn't been passed on to a visiting junior school class, who added theirs too.

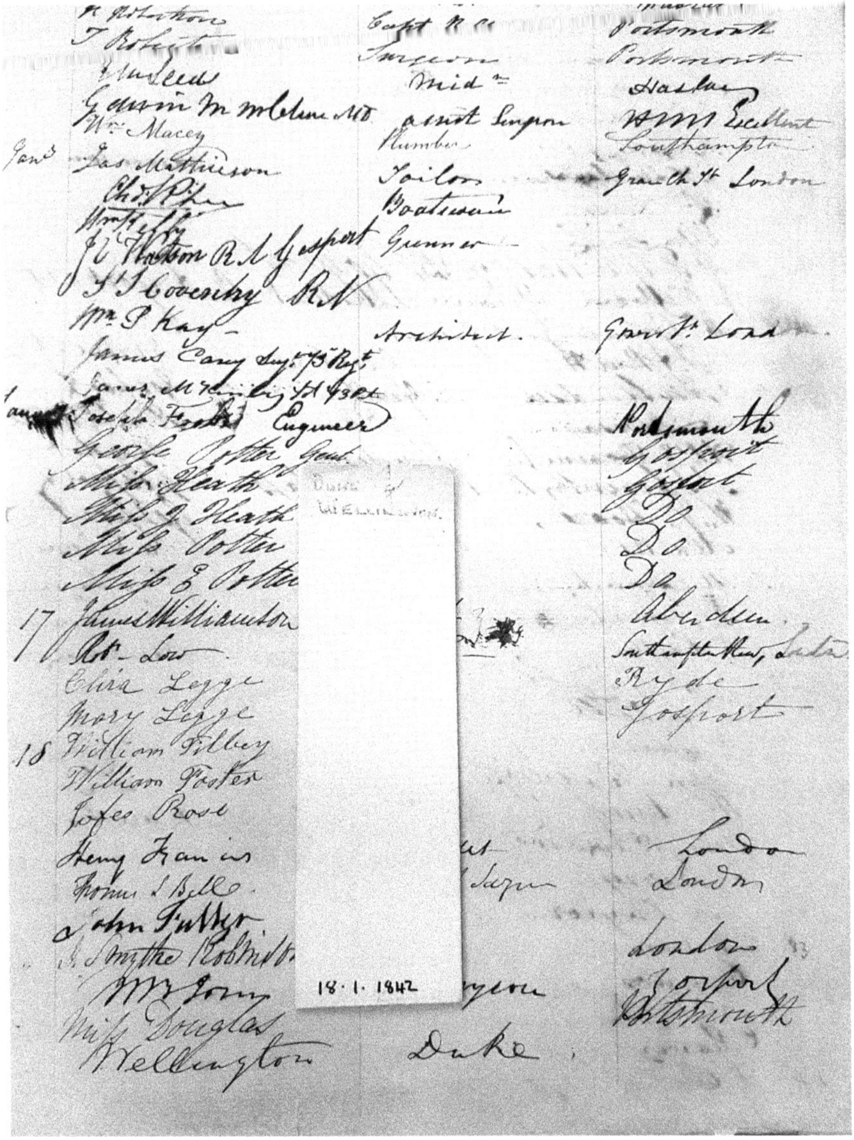

The visitors' book contains not only the signatures of famous people, including the Duke of Wellington, but also the signatures of eighteenth and nineteenth century ladies of the night brought into Haslar by surgeons and visitors themselves.

Caroline Blades

Above: Day Surgery NHS and military staff on a most happy unit.
Below: VADs attend to patients after D Day

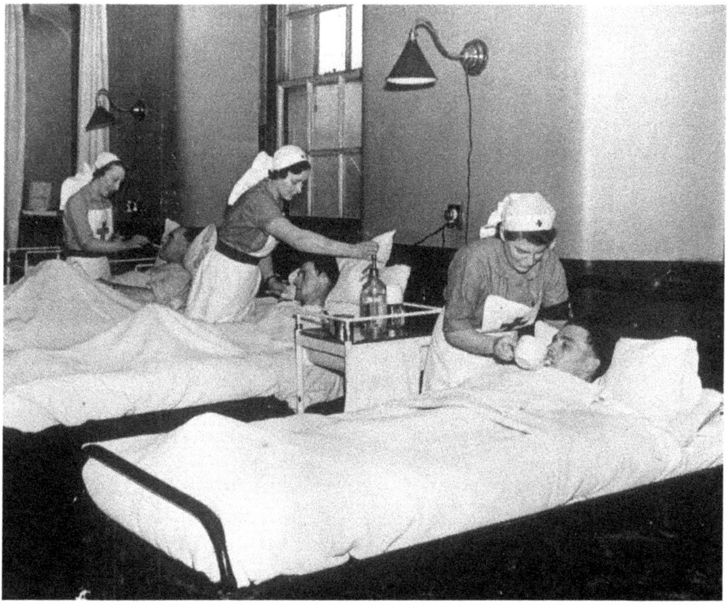

Sea Fog by Wesley Brown
www.wesleybrown.co.uk

Chapter Five
The Unexplained – Tales of the Supernatural

Since Haslar opened in 1753, death has visited on a regular basis. In the first seven years over 2,500 patients and casualties were recorded as being buried in the Paddock at Haslar. Many dead sailors and marines were brought to Haslar and marked in the muster books as 'admitted dead for burial'. Returning ships sent many crew who were suffering from disease and injury; many of them expired on the floor of the Arcade while waiting to be seen by the surgeon's Mate. A high number of Haslar's staff died from disease caught from patients and were buried on site.

From excavations of the Paddock and various areas of Haslar's grounds by forensic archaeologists from Cranfield University, it is estimated that some 8,000-20,000 are buried in the Paddock and surrounding area, with another 1,359 registered as buried in the Memorial Gardens that was the Haslar cemetery from 1826-1859.

It is only natural that tales of the spirit world abounded among hospital staff and many a joke was played on new staff over the years. The cellars were always spooky places to be at the best of times, and at night staff would often only agree to go there in pairs (maybe because of the two bodies kept in baths by the physiotherapy school for anatomy training ... or those Chinese severed heads). When on night duty, one heard many things that could not be explained, such as a dying patient saying that their family was sitting at the foot of the bed waiting to take them 'beyond'.

The Victorian press reported an incident when a doctor, called out at night to a sick officer at one of the houses in Haslar, sent a nurse with a prescription to the dispensary. It was a stormy winter's night and she wore a red cloak, drawn around a lantern. She was seen by a guard, who – on seeing this strange sight coming towards him – collapsed. He was taken to the guard house and expired within the hour.

Patients in Sick Officers Block reported seeing a Nursing Sister in grey who walked the wards tucking in patients ... strange that it was only at night. Then there was the secretary with an office in one of the Georgian houses, who walked in to see a lady dressed in Victorian style, standing behind her desk ... the image of the lady faded in seconds. You can read about many more incidents like this in this chapter.

Over the years Haslar Heritage Group and the owner of the site have been approached by TV ghost hunters and paranormal investigators, asking to visit Haslar and the answer has always been no: if there are spirits, then let them lie.

On the path to the church

I was a serving MOD Police Officer stationed at Fort Blockhouse / Haslar from April 1998 to April 2004. During that time various unexplained supernatural events happened. One in particular I wrote about for a competition in a MOD newspaper, for which I won the Star Prize, a camera.

This is what I wrote:

It was 10.15pm on a very warm summer's evening during the latter part of July 2003. I had been on duty for a little over three hours, and was carrying out foot patrol of Haslar. I had just left the Accident Treatment Centre, having checked that it was all secure.

I walked over to the path that leads to St Luke's church and there was a fox cub playing on the grass to my right, chasing moths. As I stopped to watch this, I realised I was not alone: about 20 feet further up the path was an old lady walking slowly towards the entrance to the church. She was leaning slightly and was about 5' to 5'5" tall and of small build. She was wearing a knee-length light brown coat.

As I carried on with my patrol, I passed within 10 feet of her, and could plainly see that she looked old and frail. As I walked alongside the church to go and check that the rear office door was locked, I began to think about the old lady: she couldn't have come from the Accident Treatment Centre as it had been shut since just after 9pm, so maybe she had come from one of the wards, but it was a bit late for a patient to be walking around. And then I thought maybe she had a relative in the hospital who was possibly dying, or had died, and that she wanted to spend some time in the church.

After I checked that the rear door was locked, I decided to go and see if the woman was OK. As I returned to the church main door I could see no sign of her. It had taken less than a minute to check the door, and the cub was still playing on the grass. On entering the church I could see that she was not in there and there was nowhere else she could have gone. Back outside again I had a quick look around but could not find her, so I walked up to the main entrance and asked the Main Gate guard if he had seen anyone. He informed me that the only person he had seen in the last half hour was the mortician who had been called in.

I then telephoned the Patient Services Centre to see if they had any reports of a lady missing from a ward, but they hadn't and there were no visitors either.

Where had this lady come from and – more importantly – where had she gone?

About an hour later, the mortician came into reception to hand in the mortuary keys, and we started talking about the body he had just been dealing with. He told me that it was a frail old lady of 96 years. I asked him about her height and build to which he replied that she had been about five feet tall and small. As he told me this, all the hairs on my arms and neck stood up and the Main Gate guard said that the colour drained from my face.

Had I had my first encounter with one of the permanent residents of Haslar Hospital?

__Adie Denyer__

An eerie night with the water tower standing sentinel

On a cold winter's night ...

A windy winter's night midway through night duty on E4 ward. Me and Taff Thomas were sitting comfortably in our chairs; it had gone midnight, and we had an arrangement that one of us would sleep for an hour while the other stayed awake, then we would change over. We knew that there would be rounds without any notice by either the Duty Sister or Duty Chief, and even by the Duty Matron on the rare occasion.

I was reading my book and Taff was asleep when suddenly the doors at the entrance to the ward swung open. I kicked Taff to wake him up. We both looked at the door: nobody had entered the ward but there was a cold atmosphere in the area.

Taff went back to sleep. I continued to read.

Brendan Hynes

Footsteps on the parquet floor

In 1971 I was a Probationary Medical Technical Nurse on night duty on what was then E4 ward (at the time of closing Haslar it was A4 ward).

When on duty, night staff invariably wore slippers or plimsolls. This was so as to not disturb the patients as we walked the wards at night.

This was especially important on E Block as some, if not all, of the four wards there had hollow parquet floors and outdoor shoes sounded louder on them than on a normal floor.

The wards received regular visits at night from the Receiving Room (A&E) Staff, the Block Night Nursing Sister, and occasionally the Hospital matron to make sure that all was well and all the staff were awake.

When someone entered the ward it was customary and expected that the ward staff would stand up and that the senior would give their name and Rating. They would then report the number of patients and that all was well or give an update on any occurrence of note.

I was on night duty on my own. The ward was only half full, it was possibly a weekend and was in any case a quiet medical ward. I was sitting at the desk at the top end of the long Florence Nightingale type ward with a couple of the old-fashioned concertina folding screens around my desk which shielded the patients somewhat from the Angle poise lamp that I was using. I was reading a novel.

Suddenly the heavy swing doors at the far end (the St Luke's Church end) of the ward swung heavily and noisily open, something that no-one would do on night duty.

Heavy footsteps walked down the long ward – I had time to wonder what sort of idiot this was!

As usual if anyone on official duty entered the ward from that end I could not see them because of the screens and the desk light in my eyes, so I waited until the footsteps sounded about a dozen feet away and then stood up to attention to 'report the ward'.

At the instant my eyes cleared the top of the screens the footsteps stopped ... there was no-one there!

Every hair on the back of my neck stood on end and I was gone – in seconds I was up two flights of stairs to E5 ward where there was a Medical Assistant and a Naval Nurse on duty. I asked the Medical Assistant to come down with me and we searched the ward. No one was there who shouldn't have been and none of the patients had been woken or disturbed.

I have thought about the incidents many times and am convinced I encountered a hospital ghost.

Sometimes we young folk would play tricks on each other, but of course the best part of a successful prank was after everyone had enjoyed it to let the 'victim' know they had been conned.

No-one ever said anything about it to me – and E Block, like many other places in Haslar, was known to be haunted.

So, unless I dreamed it, although I am sure that I was wide awake, I have always put it down to one of Haslar's long-gone staff or patients walking 'their' ward.

Needless to say, for the rest of that night and my remaining night duty on E4 I moved my desk and chair nearer to the exit at my end of the ward. But my visitor never visited me again.

David Rawson

Ghostly rattling of tea-cups

I have very fond memories of Haslar hospital both as a patient and a member of staff. I was one of the fortunate people (if fortunate is the right word) to be able to use the extensive services available at this wonderful hospital. I had the benefit of podiatry, physiotherapy, X-rays, surgery, several visits to A&E and numerous outpatient appointments for various ailments.

I decided in 2007 to work for the NHS and secured a job on E6 Orthopaedic ward at Haslar. I spent just over two years there as a Health Care Support Worker until it closed. It was like being part of a large family, as people you didn't even know – staff, patients and visitors – would say 'good morning' to you in the corridors or give you a smile. This is lost in a bigger hospital.

While I worked there, there were several areas of the hospital that were a bit creepy to visit on your own, especially the equipment library which was in the basement. We used to try and go there in pairs, making out that the equipment was too heavy to carry back on your own. But sometimes it was just because it was in a very quiet and usually deserted area of the hospital and we were scared that something might happen to us, as we had all heard about the Haslar ghosts.

My ward – E6 – was moved for a while to another ward in the hospital that had been closed for some time, for some work to be carried out on it. On some night shifts we used to hear what sounded like the rattling of cups on a tea trolley upstairs in the early hours of the morning around 4am, but knew this was not possible. Several of us heard it on more than one night. So what was it that we heard? None of us dared to go upstairs to find out, so we put it down to a supernatural phenomenon. We were glad to move back to our old ward as soon as it was ready.

Sue Lawman

The oval staircase built in 1957 and not loved by some who had to use it

A disappearing act

I thought I once saw a ghost at Haslar walking around the building. I used to work there in the operating theatres and got there early for a Saturday waiting list. I was half asleep as I parked my car but as I looked up after walking towards the building I saw someone was walking about 40-50 yards in front of me. They walked around the side of the building; I was close behind but when I got round the corner they had vanished. There is nowhere they could have gone. I looked for every option but there wasn't one – they had simply disappeared. They were wearing what looked like a long, dark military coat down to the knees. I was wary anyway, as no-one else was around, it was dark and the character didn't look right in terms of their appearance for that time of day.

When they disappeared I turned round and went to another entrance to the hospital. I was too scared to go any further in that direction. It spooked me out for a while but other people I worked with had ghost stories too so it made me feel better. This was in about 2004.

Dean Rutter

A sigh like a last breath

I was doing nights on F3 ward Genito Urinary. It was all quiet about three or four o'clock in the morning and I could hear this strange breathing noise, like the last breaths of a dying patient, but there was no patient in that part of the ward. I checked all the patients: nothing, but still this long drawn-out sigh like a last breath. I couldn't work it out.

This went on for several nights until one morning I was getting things ready for breakfast and out the corner of my eye I saw a spout of steam go up in the gunboat yard. A couple of seconds later I heard the sigh. I checked again: the spout of steam then after a couple of seconds, the sigh. It was the sound of the steam relief valve travelling along the water pipes and being amplified by the ward radiator. Another ghost laid.

Alan Herbert

Pranks and fool's errands

I served at Haslar from 1987 to 1990. On my first night shift, staff would 'kindly' regale the various ghost stories passed down through time, because I was a student nurse. Then they'd send me on a fool's errand to some dark, isolated corner of the hospital or to the mortuary for a laugh.

There would be inter-ward pranks involving white sheets, capes, nurses' caps and drip stands.

There were some genuinely unexplained stories involving call buttons going off on dark deserted wards (F block, for example), patients seeing a matron, seen walking through the ward and then disappearing, and strange noises from departments locked up for the night with no staff around. The attics above E block were exorcised by a chaplain due to unexplained noises heard at night.

I never minded working nights but didn't like having to walk the corridors on my own.

Laura Way (née Mortimer)

Behind the locked door

During 2008 and 2009, a lot of the nursing staff and doctors had to work at St Mary's Dermatology for a couple of days each week, which left just the two Admin staff on the Unit. A naval chap used to come up from Pathology to collect specimens each day, but on this particular day we did not have any (no clinic having being held the day before).

He could not find the Admin staff to ask where the specimens were, so he wandered on down to the end of the corridor looking for us. He could hear voices but the door was locked and no-one answered his call.

On the way back he realised we were both in the office at the top of the stairs. We assured him that there was no-one down that end, nor in the Ward opposite, but he said it was definitely a man and a woman that he had heard; he had assumed they were doctor and patient. In the end we had to take him back down there, open the door in question and show him that we just kept stock in the room.

Maureen Bennett

The music box from another world

I frequently used Haslar, due to my son and I being disabled. The first spooky experiences happened in 1993 when my son was 19 months old and in the children's ward. He was really unwell and had a room of his own. He went for tests and I went for a walk during that time. I went back onto the ward to wait for him and as I entered the room, I saw a little girl (around 4-5 years old) in a white nightdress, sitting on the floor of my boy's room, dramatically crying. As I went to talk to her she shuffled under the bed.

I went to fetch a nurse and when I got back, the little girl had gone. The nurse said she didn't know who it was. Later that day, I had dozed in the chair next to my son (who was sleeping) and was woken by the same crying noise. When I looked, the same girl was standing looking out the window and although she was making the distressed crying noise, I couldn't see her face and she didn't act like she was wiping any tears. She had shoulder-length straggly hair and was wearing the same nightdress (to the floor) with tie ribbon at the top. I called to her to see if she was OK and asked her name … no response. I got up to walk round the bed towards her and she ran – through the bed, through the wall and in the direction of corridor.

I was not afraid, but went into the corridor to see if I could follow her to find out more. As I looked I saw her facing the corridor wall crying. At the same time a nurse came along and asked if all OK. I said yes but that I was watching a special child (I didn't want to use the word 'spirit'). She nodded and went on. Lots of people passed this child but nobody reacted and the girl stayed where she was, still crying.

Another nurse asked if I was alright. I said yes, whilst watching the 'child' and the nurse said "Oh, you've seen our friend." I nodded. She said: "Approach her, she's no harm." As I got close, the girl turned and ran across the corridor and disappeared. The place she disappeared was through a solid wall again.

In the three weeks I was there with my son, I often heard her crying but only saw her three times (and never again in my son's room). When talking to the nurse, she said it was believed the girl was a very sick child who was admitted into the ward years before; while she was in there, her Mum became very sick (with the same illness) and had collapsed and died. The child had cried hysterically for days, wanting her mum but not knowing she had died.

The girl died the following day, but it seemed her spirit was still there crying for her mum.

During the same stay, on children's ward, we kept hearing a music box play a beautiful tune. On enquiring about it, a member of staff said: "If you follow the music you won't find the box, as it is a mystery."

Walking up the corridor one day, I heard the music and it sounded like it was coming from a room. The door was open and it was a storage cupboard: the music was beautiful, but there was no box to be seen. A physio said nobody knew about this box or the story behind it, but many people commented that the beautiful music was relaxing. Every time we stayed on this ward, I heard it.

While visiting the church there during a tour (after the hospital had closed), we all left the church and the man went to shut the door. I said: "What about the lady who is still sitting in the pew?" He opened the door again and I saw the lady was now standing … but I couldn't see anything from her waist down! I said: "Oh, my mistake" as I watched this lady disappear through the side wall.

Julie Carvell

The man who wasn't there

I was the personal secretary to the Head of Paediatrics at Haslar in 1996 when I had my 'spooky' experience. My office had only one entrance door from the waiting room. I was on the telephone when I saw a man come in the door and pass behind me – he was very short and was wearing black clothing and a hat. I finished the phone call and turned to speak to him … but he wasn't there!

I went into the waiting room and asked the nurse if she had seen him and she said no-one had come in. As we were on the top floor it wasn't a place where anyone would come by mistake and there was no clinic going on.

Later that day I spoke to Mrs Alison Barclay, the Play Specialist, and recounted the story.

"Oh I'm so glad you have seen him," she said. "I have seen him too."

Mrs Barclay told me that she had researched sightings such as this and the explanation she had found was that the floor levels had been changed over the years and therefore the 'ghosts' walked on the original levels, thus appearing to be short.

Shirley Allen

A gruesome murder

It was rumoured that our nurses' block was haunted by the ghost of a Nursing Sister who appeared in the lift at the end of the corridor. It had once been the psychiatric wing before it became nurses' quarters.

We were told when we joined up about a Sister who was taking a patient upstairs to the ward when she was strangled in the lift. It made us afraid to go to the 'heads' at night. Also stories of a ghost Sister coming around on night-duty to sign the ward book.

Terri Canniford

'Attuned' to the ghosts

I worked at Haslar as a Leading Naval Nurse between 1998 and 2002 on a variety of wards but mainly on A6.

I remember vividly being a student nurse on placement on A6 and working my first night shifts. I was advised to use a room at the far end of the ward so I could study during quieter periods and one night, at around 3am, I heard a great commotion on the floor above, trolleys being wheeled, footsteps running and raised voices. I thought a patient might have had a cardiac arrest, so I instinctively came out of the room where I was studying and went up the spiral staircase which led up to the next floor to see if I could go and help with anything, only to find myself in front of a boarded-up door at the top of the staircase in complete darkness with total silence.

At that point my body must have shut down as all I remember next is frantically running back through A6 to the ward sister's office and (hysterically) asking the staff nurses on duty which ward was upstairs. It was at that point they told me that it was a very old ward that had been 'mothballed' and not used for many years. When I explained the noises I was told it happened often and I must be 'attuned' to the ghosts of past staff and patients that resided there. Needless to say, I studied in the staff room from then on!

From that time on, I experienced all sorts of strange occurrences – patients describing a 'nursing sister' sitting at the end of their bed (they were able to describe her uniform in detail and it matched those worn many years earlier), a baby's swinging crib eerily rocking in a deserted room, and a figure of a nursing sister in the lift with only the area above her knees visible (I since found out a Sister had fallen and died in the lift shaft at a time before the floors were raised). Most vivid was a night when I and many of my nursing colleagues around the hospital heard screams and wailing voices coming from the 'Quadrangle' during the time it was being dug up and seemingly disturbing the souls of thousands of people who had died and were buried in that area.

Aside from the spooky memories Haslar was an amazing hospital, steeped in history and it was an honour to serve there as a member of the QARNNS.

Gill Heywood (née Green)

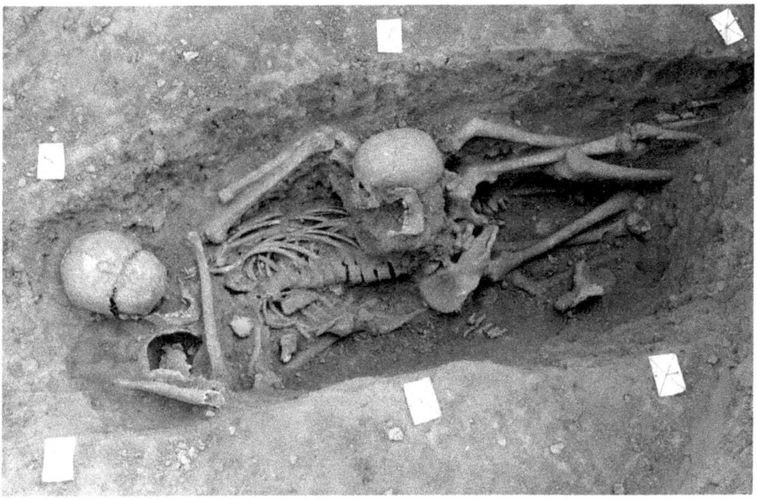

An excavated grave found in 2005 in the Paddock and containing three skeletons

Tri-Service Staff

AFTERWORD

Changes accelerated Haslar's decline

When I joined the Royal Navy in 1976, Haslar was one of nine military hospitals in the UK and when I first worked there in the 1980s it was a bustling place, not only training Royal Navy nurses and medics, but also providing many of the District General Hospital services for the people of Gosport.

Unfortunately, in the ensuing 20 or so years, its range of specialities was decreasing at the same time that the NHS was increasing its demands for hospitals to provide a comprehensive suite of specialities to support patient care. By the time that the doors of Haslar closed, it was a ghost of its former self, unable to even meet the training demands of the Defence Medical Services, far less provide the modern, comprehensive hospital care needs of the local population.

In 1994 when the Medical Director General (Naval), Surgeon Rear Admiral Anthony Revell, called an open meeting in the gym at Haslar, I was a Surgeon Commander working at the Institute of Naval Medicine. Rear Admiral Revell confirmed that the decision had been made that the Defence Medical Services were going to reduce to one tri-Service core hospital in the UK and that the three existing single-Service hospitals would be in competition.

Admiral Revell – who was shortly to become the Surgeon General – advised us that he firmly believed that Haslar was the best option and said he would make the case when he was Surgeon General for it to be selected as the core tri-Service hospital.

All three Services fought for their hospital to be selected but, ultimately, it was indeed Haslar's case that was judged to be the most persuasive and in 1996 it became the tri-Service Hospital – as the Royal Hospital Haslar. It would be fair to say that not everyone in the other two Services was content with the decision – it is widely believed that one of the Director Generals of the Army Services during this period pointedly never visited Haslar despite many of his Army Medical Services personnel being trained and employed there. Despite this, most personnel from across the three Services quickly settled into Haslar and many grew to love it.

The Defence Medical Services were increasingly working to deliver hospital-based medical care in the UK in partnership with the NHS, while focusing on training and preparing their military medical personnel for delivering acute deployed medical care on operations. Consequently, concerns about the long-term future of Haslar were first raised in 1998.

As part of the partnership with Portsmouth Hospitals Trust, acute care services were being delivered from the Haslar site and from the Queen Alexandra site. However, as part of Portsmouth NHS Hospitals Trust's plan to take advantage of the Private Finance Initiative being pushed by the then Chancellor of the Exchequer, Gordon Brown (a plan that was also supported by Fareham and Gosport Primary Care Trust) and to then apply for Foundation Trust status, it transferred all acute clinical care to QA. Haslar quickly lost its training status for the acute care specialities that are essential to provide the core skills for deployed military medical hospital personnel. Increasingly such personnel had to be moved to either QA or to another NHS hospital to maintain and develop their skills. Inevitably, this accelerated Haslar's decline.

The Defence Medical Services recognised they needed to develop a core hospital facility and centre for defence medicine, where they could guarantee their ability to provide the required training environment and ethos to deliver world-class deployed operational medical capability. After considerable debate within the Ministry of Defence, it was decided to seek to establish a new partnership with a suitable NHS Trust. EU legislation required the Ministry to put together an open tender to all NHS Trusts in the UK.

To the surprise of many within the Ministry, Portsmouth Hospitals Trust chose not to participate in the process and consequently did not raise an expression of interest. Over time, the bidding process was whittled down to four hospitals across the UK and, ultimately, the successful Trust was the University Hospital Birmingham Trust, which was also pursuing a Private Finance Initiative that would fund new buildings, into the design of which they incorporated a military medical unit. Birmingham achieved Foundation Trust status a few years later; it is now one of 27 designated Major Trauma Centres in England and the receiving hospital for military casualties from across the globe. The Major Trauma Centre for this part of South Hampshire is the University Hospital Southampton NHS Foundation Trust.

Portsmouth NHS Hospitals Trust currently remains the largest of the five Ministry of Defence hospital units with 260 staff from the Defence Medical Services. At the time of writing, it has yet to apply for Foundation Trust status.

Philip Raffaelli

Save Haslar Task Force

On 14 December 1998, the Ministry of Defence announced that the Royal Naval Hospital, Haslar was likely to close in 2002 under a sweeping review of defence medical services. Haslar's role since the eighteenth century had been to care for sick and wounded seaman; its modern role was as a training hospital for the military, and also as the first receiving station for troop casualties returning from overseas. It had a modern civilian role as well, including accident and emergency and orthopaedic services for 110,000 patients every year. Around £25 million had recently been spent modernising the facilities there. The possible loss of this busy District General Hospital was a massive shock to local people and sparked one of the greatest and longest campaigns to save a hospital this country had ever seen. The campaign was led by Gosport Borough Council who sponsored the 'Save Haslar Task Force', of which I was proud to be part.

The Task Force arranged a march for Sunday 24 January 1999 expecting 10,000 people to turn up but, on the day over 20,000 people walked the mile from Walpole Park over Haslar Bridge to the hospital gates. More than 170 police plus 50 council stewards were on hand to direct traffic and some roads had to be closed to make room for the vast crowd. It took the protesters nearly an hour and a half to walk past the old Haslar gate to make their views known. Immediately after the march there were encouraging vibes from the government regarding the future of the hospital, especially after Health Minister Frank Dobson visited Haslar. However, after further meetings with him and the Defence Minister, George Robertson, it became clear that it would be unlikely that we would save the hospital but, with a sustained campaign, we could ensure it stayed open until new facilities were in place. These would be for the military in Birmingham and for civilians at Queen Alexandra Hospital in Cosham.

The Save Haslar Task Force decided to keep up the pressure on the government to make sure the arbitrary and dangerous closing of the site in 2002 would not take place before adequate replacement facilities were provided for both the country's military, and also the local population across the south.

To end on an ironic personal note, I had left for the demonstration to 10 Downing Street after being told my mother-in-law had just died at Gosport's War Memorial Hospital and returned to the news that my eldest sister, Marjorie, had died at Haslar Hospital on the same day.

Such is life!

Peter Edgar

Haslar keeps on giving

'Farm For Life' is a charity created by Lloyd and Karen Clever in 2007, which they run from their home in Stubbington. It aims to plant 'positive seeds' in developing countries. In August 2015, in a casual conversation, a friend mentioned that there was a lot of 'kit' left in Haslar that might be of use to their charity. The developers gave Lloyd and Karen permission to remove free-standing equipment from the building.

Lloyd and some helpers started removing beds, chairs, cabinets, X-ray readers, and other odds and ends, including the biggest pile of crutches and walking aids I have ever seen. Initially, some of the equipment was offered to the NHS and other UK charities, but they had no need of such things at the time. So, the kit is bound for Sierra Leone, Ghana and the Gambia, where a notional sum is charged for it – Lloyd believes that this is better than giving it away entirely free of charge, because the countries then value the equipment more.

Lloyd says that Haslar buildings have now become the home of wildlife, with foxes running in the wards, pigeons inhabiting the upper areas and feral cats having the time of their lives.

The developers of the Haslar site have given the charity use of a store, just to the left as you enter the old main gate from HMS *Dolphin*. In additional to wheelchairs and crutches, the store holds furniture, educational items, tools and also sports equipment donated by the University of Southampton.

David Gary

Life and energy

The master plan provides for the redevelopment of the entire site to create a residential community with healthcare, retail, leisure and hospitality forming an integral part of the development. It proposes to restore to Haslar some of that life and energy that once reverberated through the many beautiful and historic buildings on the site. The plan encompasses a mixed-use scheme with care and health at its centre. These facilities will be shared by the retirement community, the residents and the public, creating a broad and vibrant community.

Stephen Burke, Harcourt Developments

A restorative quality

As a child growing up locally, friends and family had been through the doors of Haslar as patients. When I became Gosport's MP in 2010 the site had already been sold and I inherited a constituency still mourning the loss of this well-loved hospital. Now, I am lucky enough to live here at Haslar and to witness first-hand the next page in the long history of this great site. It is an addictive place to live. The grounds are supremely beautiful and tranquil. I find a restorative, almost nourishing, quality in the gardens and miss it terribly when I am away. The house is an adventure; I love living here but cannot help feeling very much a temporary custodian – it is as if I have a small walk-on part in its rich and colourful story.

Caroline Dinenage

Royal Marine Band, Portsmouth, marking the beginning of the end and the closure of Haslar

Acknowledgements

The compilers and Chaplin Books would like to thank Haslar Heritage Group for kindly making available photographs from their archive; Wesley Brown for permission to use his picture of Haslar in the sea-mist; Andrew Wing for permission to reproduce his cartoon of staff at Haslar on pages 24-25; Barry Prosser for his depictions of nursing staff and medical assistants on pages 116-117; Charles Swain for the back cover photograph of Haslar illuminated at night; Gosport Discovery Centre; the office of the Mayor of New York; the QARNNS Archive; and Ted Grant, author of 'The Toothwright's Tale' for permission to use an extract from Surgeon Commander Timothy Hall's memories of Haslar that appear in that book

This book would not have been possible without so many people taking time to write to us with their memories of Haslar:

Christine Allen (née Loader)
Shirley Allen
Lynn Allison
Betty Archer
Terry Archer
Margaret Ball
Doug Barlow
Bob Beckwith
Sylvia Bell (née Feetey)
Maureen Bennett
Caroline Blades (née Souter)
Bob Bottriell
Jackie Bradbury
Jane Brewer
Jacky Broadbent
Jacqui Brooks (née Jones)
Rosemary Brooks
John Bull
Hilary Butterworth
Terri Canniford
Julie Carvel
June Chambers
Mark Chapman
Caroline Churcher
Sally Cleal
Andrew Cousins
Margaret Cowell
Douglas Cramp
Laura Cranley
Ron Cross
Rachel Daly
Pauline Daniels (née Robson)
Stephen Davies
Mark Davis
Adie Denyer
Lynne Derry
Caroline Dinenage
Paul Dodd
Trudie Doughty
Glenn Duggan
Bill Durning
Peter Edgar
Rob England
Hilary Essam
Maggie Feist
Bill Fewtrell
Rosemary Fost
Richard Franklin
Dave Fry
Brian Furlong

Panoecia Gaunt (née Foster)
Lorraine Gee
Gill Grove (née Hicks)
Jane Hahn (née Baker)
Mabel Halewood (née Packer)
Timothy Hall
Tony Harrington
Bob Harrop
Karen Harrop
Sue Harvey
Elizabeth Haughton
Nigel Hearnden
Tony Heath
Evelyn Mary Heffernan (née Seward)
Alan Herbert
Gill Heyward (née Green)
Bob Hillier
Sue Hitchman
Nigel Hockenhull
Lesley Holmes (née Daley)
Derek Howard
Lyn Howard
Sally Hughes
Jeanette Hunter (née Read)
Lena Hutton (née Scoular)
Brendan Hynes
Mark Jackson
Bobbie Johnson (née Cox)
Edith Kinghorn
Tom Ladd
Sue Lawman
Caroline Lee
Marian Lee
Maxine Leyland
Helen Long
Evelyn Love
Nicola Maasdam
Nick Martin
Radiance McLaren-Draper
Rita Muston
Rod Newman
Andrew Newton
Guy Nicholls
Shane O'Leary
Marilyn Paternotte
Louise Paterson
Frances Patter
Chris Pearce
Tony Pearce
Simon Pearce
Jacqueline Pearson
Bridget Pelling
Alan Petrie
Veronica Phillips
Rick Pittard
Alan Prior
Barry Prosser
Philip Raffaelli
Michael Raven
David Rawson
John 'Scouse' Redmond
Louise Reece
Penny Reeves
Karl Rich
Sue Richards (née Price)
Rita Rideout (née Higgins)
Sheila Rightson
Mark Robberts
Sarah Robins
John Roffey
Cheryl Rolls (née Churcher)
Dean Rutter
Lorraine Scaife
Ellen Seward (née Kirtley)
Gill Sickling
Peter Simpson
Howard Staniforth
Victoria Stewart (née Laughton)
Bill Swinfield
Steve Sykes
Eddie Taylor
Tony Thatcher
Pamela Tree
Laura Way (née Mortimer)
Berny Webster
Kerry Webster
Sarah Wilde
Sandy Williams
Pete Williamson
Catherine Wilson
Emma Woolley
Michael Wright
Sylvia Wrightson
Colin Young

About The Compilers

Eric Birbeck MVO (*right below*) served in the Royal Naval Medical Service for 32 years with Haslar as his alma mater. He then served at Haslar as a Technical Officer for a further 12 years, during which time he co-founded Haslar Heritage Group in 2001. He now conducts historical research into Haslar and is the author of a number of books and papers on Haslar. In 2007 he was appointed a Member of the Royal Victorian Order for services to Her Majesty the Queen.

David Gary (*left below*) grew up in Basingstoke before joining the Royal Navy. He served for ten years in the Writer branch, after which he worked for local government. His time in local government ended in Taunton, where he and his wife had also run a smallholding and a local village store. He studied at the Universities of Exeter and Plymouth to gain an MBA. After eight years in Spain, he returned to the UK and is the compiler of *Going Over the Water: Memories of the Gosport Ferry*, which was published by Chaplin Books in 2016.

ALSO FROM CHAPLIN BOOKS:

Going Over the Water: Memories of the Gosport Ferry compiled by David Gary

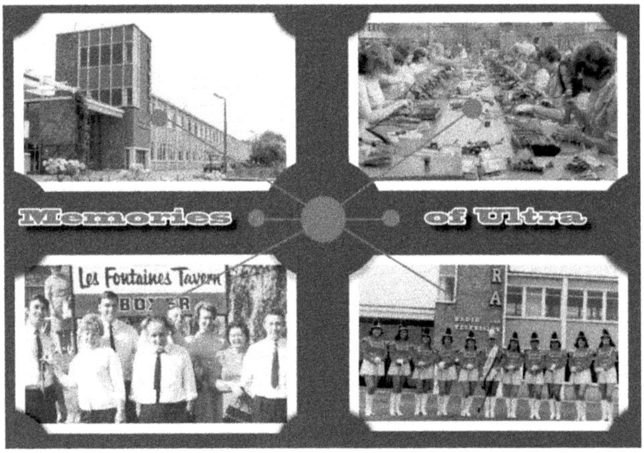

Memories of Ultra, compiled by Geoff O'Neill and Mick Laming

HMS Ganges Days by Peter Broadbent

Lightning Source UK Ltd.
Milton Keynes UK
UKHW020904191119
353823UK00006B/635/P

9 781911 105466